HIS
PROMISED
LAND

THE AUTOBIOGRAPHY OF

JOHN P. PARKER,

FORMER SLAVE AND CONDUCTOR

ON THE UNDERGROUND RAILROAD

HIS PROMISED LAND

EDITED BY STUART SEELY SPRAGUE

W. W. Norton & Company

NEW YORK · LONDON

Copyright © 1996 by The John P. Parker Historical Society

Printed in the United States of America
First published as a Norton paperback 1998
Excerpt from Frank Moody Gregg Papers, MSS 265
is by permission of the Ohio Historical Society.
For information about permission to reproduce selections
from this book, write to Permissions,
W. W. Norton & Company, Inc., 500 Fifth Avenue, New York, NY 10110.
The text of this book is composed in Garamond No 3
with the display set in Caslon Antique
Composition and manufacturing by The Maple-Vail Book Manufacturing Group.
Book design by Jam Design

Library of Congress Cataloging-in-Publication Data

Parker, John P., 1827–1900.
His promised land : the autobiography of John P. Parker, former
slave and conductor on the underground railroad / edited by Stuart Sprague.
p. cm.
ISBN 0-393-03941-2
1. Parker, John P., 1827–1900. 2. Slaves—Southern States—
Biography. 3. Freedmen—Biography. 4. Afro-American
abolitionists—Biography. 5. Underground railroad. I. Sprague,
Stuart, 1937– . II. Title.
E450.P238 1996
975.004'96073'0092—dc20   96-14570
CIP

ISBN 0-393-31718-8 pbk.

W. W. Norton & Company, Inc.
500 Fifth Avenue, New York, N.Y. 10110
www.wwnorton.com

W. W. Norton & Company Ltd.
Castle House, 75/76 Wells Street, London W1T 3QT

1 2 3 4 5 6 7 8 9 0

Contents

Preface

A BRIEF BIOGRAPHICAL SKETCH

JOHN P. PARKER was born into slavery in Norfolk, Virginia, in 1827, the son of a black woman and a white man.[1] At the age of eight, Parker was bound to another slave and forced to walk from Norfolk to Richmond, where he was then sold and marched in chains to Mobile, Alabama. In his oral history, Parker recounts his memories of this brutal journey to Mobile: his hatred of captivity, and the solace he found in helping another slave weaker than him. His rage and resourcefulness served him again and again when he later became a conductor on the Underground Railroad, helping hundreds of slaves escape to freedom.[2]

It took Parker eighteen years to acquire his own freedom. He was owned for many years by a Mobile doctor.[3] Parker remembers that the boys in the family smuggled books to him, and that the doctor encouraged him to learn the trade of iron moulding. After Parker attempted to escape, though, the doctor decided to sell him as a field hand. Saving himself from hard labor on a sugar plantation, Parker persuaded a widowed patient of the doctor's to purchase him for $1,800. Parker's reputation for stubborness was perhaps why the price of his freedom was set unusually high. He paid the widow back over the course of a year and a half, using his skills in the foundry to earn money. In 1845, Parker became a free man.

Moving first to New Albany, Indiana, and then to Cincinnati, Ohio, Parker began boarding with a barber who hoped to rescue his own family from slavery. Parker was initially reluctant to join the man in his endeavor, but eventually, although the barber himself gave up in despair, Parker managed to rescue the family—the first in a long string of successes. In 1848, Parker started his own family, marrying Miranda Boulden, a Cincinnati native, and establishing a small general store at Beechwood Factory, Ohio.

The next year, Parker and his wife moved to Ripley, Ohio, then a bustling river town with a thriving abolitionist community (the Ripley Abolition Society had a membership of over 300). In Ripley, Parker could work at his profession in ironworks and continue to help slaves escape. Many anti-slavery southerners, particularly a number of ministers, had chosen or been forced to leave the South and had relocated to this area along the Ohio River. Ripley was home to two "Negro settlements," which had been created thirty years before Parker's arrival as places for the emancipated slaves of planter Samuel Gist.[4] Ohio's first abolitionist, U.S. Senator Alexander Campbell, also lived in Ripley, as did the Reverend John Rankin, whose hilltop home served as a beacon to escaping slaves. Rankin's house allegedly sheltered the woman who inspired Harriet Beecher Stowe's "Eliza," whose harrowing night passage across the thawing Ohio River, leaping from one ice patch to the next with her baby in her arms, is vividly described in *Uncle Tom's Cabin*.

To reach Ripley, fugitives often followed the Maysville road, which connected the slave-rich bluegrass region centered in Lexington, Kentucky with the Ohio River. Maysville, the largest town in northeastern Kentucky, had an early anti-slavery society. On the other side of the river, a few miles north of Ripley, lay the town of Red Oak, where the Reverend James Gilliland and his congregation formed the core of the largest concentration of Underground Railroad conductors in Ohio.[5] These borderlands in Ohio sustained the busiest terminals on the entire Underground Railroad, possibly even providing the railroad with its name. According to W. M. Mitchell's 1860 *The Underground Railroad,* the term originated in 1831 when Tice Davis swam across the Ohio, barely eluding his former master. Furious, the slaveowner is said to have exclaimed, "The damned abolitionists must have a railroad by which they run off" slaves.

For nearly fifteen years, John P. Parker rescued fugitive slaves, leading the *Cincinnati Commercial Tribune* to write, shortly after Parker's death, "a more fearless creature never lived. He gloried in danger. . . . He would go boldly over into the enemy's camp and filch the fugitives to freedom." The inherent danger of aiding slaves was much greater for an African-American who, if caught, would receive a lengthy jail term, providing he survived pursuit without being shot dead. When the Civil War broke out, he smuggled a few hundred slaves into the service of the Union Army, a record admired in the 1883 *History of Brown County, Ohio:* "It is but a word of justice to say of Mr. Parker's service during the late war, that the half could not be told."

Parker led a dual life—by night ferrying fugitives across the Ohio River, by day working as an iron moulder. In his oral autobiography, Parker concentrates on stories of the Underground Railroad. His work in the foundry and machine shop was also notable as was the series of inventions he patented.

In December 1865, John P. Parker and his partner William Hood purchased a foundry and blacksmith shop including its contents for $6,000. By mid-March of 1868, Parker's business and property were estimated to be worth between $8,000 and $10,000. He sought out African-American buyers and appealed to racial pride. An article entitled "Mechanic" written from Ripley, Ohio, appeared in the Little Rock *Arkansas Freeman* of October 5, 1869. In it Parker declared that "a plow made by a black man, tells for us more than a hundred first class speeches." Parker proposed sending "an Agent among the Southern people—the said Agent to be a colored man. He will ask the trade of our people in particular." Of his products he declared, "we manufacture engines, varying in sizes from ten to twenty-five horsepower; Dorsey's patent reaper and mower; and a sugar mill, which thus far has given universal satisfaction. Besides we expect this fall and winter, to get up an assortment of steel plows."

Many African-American businesspeople failed during the Panic of 1873, because of undercapitalization, hard times, and prejudice, but Parker survived. He brought in a partner to manufacture threshers as Belchamber & Parker in 1876. The firm dissolved two years later. Parker's net worth peaked at between $15,000 and $20,000 during 1882, but diminished during the economic downturn in 1883.

Parker's work diversified. By now he had developed a blacksmith shop and a machine shop, as well as a coal yard associated with his foundry. But becoming partners with a hardworking, practical miller as the firm of J. P. Parker & Kirkpatrick brought him grief. They shared an investment in the Model Mill, which was bought by Kirkpatrick in August 1883.

This range of activities stretched Parker's resources to the breaking point, and, by mid-June of 1885, he was in a difficult financial situation. His expertise in the foundry business was of no use to him in milling. Investment in milling brought Parker to the brink of bankruptcy, which was compounded by a May 1, 1886 fire that totally consumed the four-story brick building which housed the mill. The structure was insured for $6,500 and valued at $15,000.[6]

Three years later, in August of 1889, another fire that would affect Parker broke out. It started in the boiler room of the Ripley Mill & Lumber Company on Front Street near Parker's home and business. The town's steam fire engine was insufficient, and the fire spread to nearly the entire block. Parker's residence was completely destroyed and his old foundry damaged, but the fire department was able to save Parker's machine shop—a stroke of good luck since his principal business at the time was manufacturing tobacco screws for his patented tobacco presses. Parker proved resilient; by September of 1890, he had built a new foundry and woodworking shop a block and a half from his old one. The Phoenix Foundry was the largest such enterprise located between Portsmouth and Cincinnati, Ohio. Parker's son, Hale, served as the western agent for the John P. Parker tobacco press and pulverizer.[7]

This series of disasters probably explains the stipulation in Parker's will forbidding his six offspring from carrying on the family business. Far better, he thought, to have them go to college and become involved in the learned professions. In 1892, Parker told Wilbur H. Siebert, the leading Underground Railroad historian, that he expected his children to fill respected places in communities removed from the Ohio River.[8]

John P. Parker, an extensive reader, shared his love of learning with his children and must have been proud of their achievements. Two of his sons, Hale Giddings (born 1851) and Cassius Clay (1854), both named after prominent abolitionists, went through the preparatory school at Oberlin College. Hale Parker graduated from Oberlin's classical program in 1873. In 1878, Hale and his wife moved to St. Louis, where he became principal of a school for black children and went on to study law. He moved with his family to Chicago after becoming involved with the "Negro Department" of the Chicago World's Fair; his two daughters and his son all graduated from college.

Cassius Parker became a school teacher in Indiana. The youngest son, Horatio W. Parker (1856), was a principal at a school in Illinois, later moving to St. Louis, where he taught and became a clerk in the post office. Parker had three daughters, Bianca (1871), Portia (1865), and Hortense (1859), all of whom studied music.[9] In 1883, Hortense Parker was one of the first African-American graduates of Mount Holyoke College in South Hadley, Massachusetts. Like two of her brothers, she, too, moved to St. Louis where she married and taught music.

In just two generations, the Parker family moved from slavery to the college-educated black middle class. John Parker's drive and spirit brought him out of servitude and gained him a position as a businessman in his community. His courage and generosity made him one of the small group of Americans, and even smaller group of African-Americans, who helped pull other people out of slavery, even at the risk of their lives. At his death in 1900, he left a valuable legacy for both his family and his country.

THE AUTOBIOGRAPHY

WE WOULD NEVER have had John Parker's autobiography without Frank Moody Gregg's intense interest in the story of "Eliza's" flight across the thawing Ohio River in *Uncle Tom's Cabin*. Harriet Beecher's Stowe's novel, published in 1852, stirred up a great deal of controversy. From the time of its publication until the end of the nineteenth century, many people devoted vast amounts of time to validating or discrediting real-life incidents upon which Stowe might have based parts of her novel. The stories about Eliza often mentioned that she found shelter at the Reverend John Rankin's house in Ripley. Frank Moody Gregg, a native of Ripley and a reporter for the *Chattanooga News,* set out to uncover the true story.[10]

Gregg began by interviewing Rankin's son, John Rankin Jr., in Indiana and then four "corroborating witnesses," not including Parker, from Ripley. Since a fragment of the Parker autobiography discusses Eliza, it seems likely that Gregg's original purpose in visiting Parker was to continue his Eliza search, since he knew that Parker sometimes worked with the Rankins.

It appears that Parker's own story proved more engaging than whatever light he could shed on Eliza's. In Parker, Gregg found an articulate interview subject, willing to talk about a necessarily hidden subject, the secret and dangerous lives of Underground Railroad conductors. To stay out of jail and avoid retribution, white Underground Railroad conductors kept few records; there is even less documentation of the participation of African-American conductors on the Underground Railroad.[11] Gregg recognized the rare opportunity to document an African-American man's work on the Underground Railroad.

Today historians are rightly wary of accounts of black experience based on interviews given to whites. "A View from the Bottom Rail," in James West Davidson and Mark Hamilton Lytle's *After the Fact: The Art of Historical Detection* examines two interviews given by an ex-slave, Susan Hamlin.[12] The interview by an African-American and the interview by a Caucasian give remarkably different versions of the severity of slavery and the relationship between master and slave. This example of the discrepancy between narratives raises two questions about the Parker interview: Was Parker straightforward with Gregg? Did Gregg misreport what Parker said?

Parker may have slanted his account to his white audience. At the very beginning of the narrative, he states that his intelligence came from his white father. He also does not reproach his Mobile owners for their conduct. It is possible that this clemency toward white people covered an animosity rendered inexpressible by the politics of the colored line. Yet this seems less likely given the candor of the tone throughout the narrative. Parker had known both people present at the interview—Gregg and a banker friend of Parker's, Frank A. Stivers—for many years. It would have been hard for Parker to maintain a front during the many hours of this lengthy interview in front of two old acquaintances.

The question of whether Gregg misreported Parker's words is perhaps best answered by considering the manuscript's voice. Interviewers have often changed a narrator's voice to make it more consistent with written English and with the interviewer's style. Fortunately, we have another work of Gregg's to use as a standard for comparison. In early 1908, Gregg completed a typescript of his work, "The Borderland," which was a rewritten book based on Gregg's interview with Parker. The difference between the voice in the "The Borderland," and the voice in Parker's memoir becomes evident upon comparison of similar passages. Parker's language is more specific, detailed, and vivid—it has the slight rough edge associated with oral history. Consider the following two pairs of examples:

GREGG

Though the best blood of that state was in my veins, still at the age of 14, I found myself locked to a chain with others of my race, trudging along dusty highways southward.

PARKER

It was in June that I began my chainbound journey to Alabama, where I eventually reached. Our journey was long and tiresome. Imagine yourself chained to a long chain to which men, women and children were also attached. The roads were dusty or muddy.

GREGG

We were going through the mountains of Virginia. The azaleas and laurel were in full bloom, not only filled the wood with fragrance, but ran down like a flood of odor into the borders of the road. Seizing a stick, I struck at each flowering bud and sent its petals flying in every direction.

PARKER

I was trudging along a trail called a road through the mountains of Virginia. It was June. Every flower was in bloom, the wilderness was all about us, green and living. Azaleas and mountain laurels were in full bloom. Every thing seemed to be gay except myself. Picking up a stick, I struck each flowering shrub, taking delight in smashing down particularly those in bloom.

Gregg tried to remold the narrative in "The Borderland" to the genteel standards of the day. In doing so, he lost the tiny, telling details of Parker's memories, along with the emotion that Parker's account evokes. While there may have been some slight retouching by Gregg, the roughness of the presented memoir shows very little reworking. I believe that in the interview, we are close to Parker's voice, while in "The Borderland," Gregg has imposed his own. The beauty of Parker's imagery and the precision of his language is rightly attributed to Parker's own stylistic mastery and to the incredible life he lived.

A NOTE ON THE MANUSCRIPT

JOHN P. PARKER's memoir has not previously been published. In the 1880s, when Gregg originally interviewed Parker, the prevalence of racism made it difficult to publish the work. It was placed in the Duke University Archive as part of the Rankin-Parker collection—the Parker memoir, the Rankin memoir, and Gregg's "Eliza"—and accessioned on June 30, 1939.[13]

John P. Parker's lack of celebrity status and the illegibility of the manuscript may have contributed to its long delay in publication. Robert Newman and I have combined our lengthy readings and rereadings of it to present the most accurate rendition we could. Many words were deciphered from context (this is how we discovered that "mng" indicates "morning"). We have used points of ellipsis for absolutely illegible words.

Pages are missing from the original, most of them from the tenth chapter. Many of these pages can be reconstructed by substituting the corresponding passages from Gregg's "The Borderland." Asterisks have been used to indicate where this substitution begins and ends. There are two other cases of possibly missing work. The first is in a passage describing the old town of Ripley. There the pagination implies missing pages, but the narrative does not falter, which may indicate that there is a mispagination rather than that paragraphs are missing. The second possible gap involves the "Eliza" incident, and is indicated by a footnote.

All editing has been done for the sole purpose of making the work more accessible to the reader. Since the memoir was orally presented, punctuation has been somewhat changed, paragraphing has been added, capitalization has been altered for consistency, and spelling mistakes have been corrected. Where words have been added for clarification they are enclosed in brackets. We have attempted above all to preserve the spirit of the original.

—Stuart Seely Sprague

HIS
PROMISED
LAND

Original Introduction
to the Autobiography
by Frank M. Gregg

THIS IS THE story of John Parker of Ripley, Ohio. He was a mulatto with a white man's brain and imagination.[1] I knew him as a boy, as the man who was afraid to walk on the sidewalk. Winter and summer, rain or shine, he invariably walked in the middle of the street. The reason he did, was Ripley was an old town with many narrow alleys, out of which enemies could leap at him unawares. This habit he formed when there was a reward on his head, dead or alive. A courageous man, even in his old age, he was quick with his fists, a knife, or a pistol.

I sat all night with him taking and compiling the notes on which this story is based. He was a man who rarely talked, never bragged. Having made some reputation as a newspaper man, I returned to my old home town, just to talk to John Parker. I knew he had had a life of adventure, but never imagined such an interesting one as he unfolded to me and my banker friend, Frank A. Stivers, an old friend of Parker's, and the leading banker of Ripley.[2]

John Parker was born in Norfolk, Virginia, in 1827. He was only eight years old when he was sold and went to Richmond, Virginia, to live. He was chained to an old man, who was later whipped to death. This experience set the boy on fire with hatred and the desire to gain his freedom. Just four months later, he was chained to a gang of 400 slaves. It was customary at the time to sell the slaves as they passed through the country. Parker walked to the end of the slave trail at Mobile, Alabama.

When he was 14, he entered into a contract with a widow, Mrs. Ryder of Mobile.[3] If she would buy his freedom for $1,800, he would pay her back on a weekly installment plan of $10 per week with interest.[4] By this time he had made himself so disagreeable to his old master, he was glad to get rid of Parker at any price.

It was 1845 before he had paid Mrs. Ryder and gained his freedom. He was now 18, free and anxious to go north as his life had been spent as a workman in an iron foundry. He had met a free man in New Orleans who told him of the iron foundries in New Albany, Indiana. So his pass out of Mobile read to New Albany, Indiana.[5] He was there only a short time when he went to Cincinnati, thence to Ripley, Ohio, where he entered into one of the most adventurous careers of any slave runner along the entire border.

He devoted his life to forays in[to] Kentucky, to scouting on both sides of the Ohio river, to taking care of the helpless slaves who found their way to the Ohio and could not get across, to actual fighting for them as against their pursuing masters.

Owing to the stringent antislavery laws and the fugitive slave law, Parker never was to tell of his adventures. He had built up a profitable iron foundry business. He had patented a clod smashing machine which came in[to] general use.

All of his property would have been confiscated and he would have been jailed had the slave owners been able to catch him. So it behooved Parker to move with caution and silence.

These dangers did not hold him back. Almost nightly he was on the lookout for his fugitive brothers.

John Parker found kindred spirits in a group of white men, all Scotch Presbyterians, who had devoted their lives and property towards aiding and abetting the runaway slaves. It was a peculiar and friendly environment, to a degree, owing to the fact that the town of Ripley stood in the heart of the Virginia Military District of Ohio.

This district lay between the mouths of the Scioto River on the east and the Little Miami River on the west. It had been set apart by the U.S. Government for the soldiers of the Revolution of the line who were unable to locate their bounty of wild lands in the valleys of the Tennessee or the Cumberland or in the wild lands of Kentucky.

As the Ordinance of 1787 forbid slavery north of the Ohio River, this Virginia Military District of Ohio was only settled by those Virginia planters who wished to free their slaves, or to men who did not wish [to] own slaves. Two large free camps were established in the District to which southern planters would send their slaves to be freed, without their having to come with them. Then there were gathered in the District antislavery men from North and South Carolina, Tennessee, Kentucky, Pennsylvania and Virginia. The most prominent of these was Dr. Alexander Campbell, a native of Greenbrier County, [West] Virginia. [He was] the first abolitionist of Ohio, Senator from Ohio; when the British burned Washington, he rode away back to Ohio.[6] There was the Reverend John Rankin, a native of Tennessee, who according to Henry Ward Beecher brought on the Civil War.[7]

THE
AUTOBIOGRAPHY
OF
JOHN P. PARKER

ONE

I AM SPEAKING now as a man grown up, with an eternal hatred of the institution in which I found myself when I was eight years old living in Norfolk, Virginia. As a slave, all I knew was my father was one of the aristocrats of Virginia. Whoever he was, he gave me a brain which has never failed me. He also gave me imagination which was a source of comfort even in my period of despair. He gave me one more advantage: the power to hate. [1]

How I hated slavery as it fettered me, and beat me, and baffled me in my desires. But in the end that unknown ancestor of mine gave me the will and the courage to conquer or die. That's my background as the narrator of the following events of my life, which are literally true as I tell them, likewise all the things I thought both as a child and a boy as I fought daily and nightly against the pricks. It was not the physical part of slavery that made it cruel and degrading, it was the taking away from a human being the initiative, of thinking, of doing his own ways.

When I saw the old man with whom I was chained when I was a lad of eight, on our walk from Norfolk, Virginia, to

Richmond, Virginia, whom I saw beaten to death; when I was beaten by a drunken brute, with the lath in which there was a nail, and was confined to a hospital, I felt that it was the whipping of the slaves, that was its infamy.

I soon learned that there was not so much brutality in slavery as one might expect. It was an incident to the curse, but the real injury was the making of a human being an animal without hope. Now that it is all over, as I have previously stated, I know slavery's curse was not pain of the body, but the pain of the soul. Still, I can only tell of the horrible incidents that I saw and felt in order to give you the . . . [nature] of my life.

To begin with, I was sold as a child of eight, chained to an old man, walked with him from Norfolk, Virginia, to Richmond, Virginia. This old man was kind to me, he made my weight of the chain as light as he could. He talked to me kindly, because I was brokenhearted at leaving my mother. He was the only human being who was interested in me then. When we reached Richmond, I was sold to one family; he was sold to another. For some reason, which of course I never knew, this old man was severely whipped and died.

As a child I was bitterly touched with a hatred which I had to conceal, but it rankled and festered and bore its sour fruit, much to my physical disadvantage. I became obstinate and hateful, perhaps difficult to handle. Beating me only made me moody. At all events, I was still a child when I found myself sold to a trader headed south. Virginia, at this time, was merely a breeding place for the states growing rice, indigo, and cotton.

It was in June I began my chain-bound journey to Alabama, where I eventually reached. Our journey was long and tiresome. Imagine yourself chained to a long chain to which men, women, and children were also attached. The roads were dusty or muddy the June I walked in such a convoy. We met other

groups going in the same direction under the same circumstances. Some of the slaves were sullen, others gay and happy,
others were mere animals. As for me, I was designing, hateful,
and determined. Ragged and barefooted, I was resentful of the
freedom of nature.

There are only two impressions of that long journey that I
still distinctly remember. Though strongly opposite to each
other, both are indelibly fixed in my mind. The first incident
happened early in the journey. I was trudging along a trail
called a road through the mountains of Virginia. It was June.
Every flower was in bloom, the wilderness was all about us,
green and living. Azaleas and mountain laurels were in full
bloom. Every thing seemed to be gay except myself. Picking
up a stick, I struck at each flowering shrub, taking delight in
smashing down particularly those in bloom. That was my only
revenge on the things that were free.

I remember coming to a mountain brook. As the long chain
of men, women, and children crossed through the brook, I
kicked and splashed the running water. I struck at the bubbles
with my stick—anything and everything that was without
restraint was my object of wrath. As I see it now, it does not
seem possible that a boy as young as I was could conceal as
much anger as I evidently [had] against everybody and everything. I suppose that was the reason I was sold south. However, there I was like a mad bull hitting out in every direction
at my enemies.

When we came out of the brook, there was a chestnut tree
in full tasseled bloom. In the midst of the clusters sang a red
bird, to me a red blotch of blood. In an instant I had seized a
rock and with all my youth and heart of hatred, I threw it at
the red bird. It flew away careless[ly], but if it had been in my
power I would have killed [it] and been glad of the deed.
What I did do was to shake my fist at it and curse it. The rest
of the slaves laughed at my anger.

My second recollection of this long journey was a black boy Jeff. He was hitched to the caravan the fourth day out of Richmond. He was even smaller than I was, had never been away from his mother, blubbered and cried, until I kicked him to make him keep still. As my cuffing only made him cry more, I soon took pity on him.

There was another boy, larger than either Jeff or myself. One night, this big boy took Jeff's dinner, just because he was bigger and stronger. I don't think it was the stealing of Jeff's dinner that enraged me so much as the fact that he was stronger and used his power against his weaker comrade. Whatever it was, I was on him like a hawk, pummeling and clawing him, until he was glad to release Jeff's dinner.

From that time forward, I was the champion of the weak. I had found a way to beat at the "might is right" policy, which had enslaved me. As a child, I had not worked my plan out through any mental process. It was just animal plus human hatred.

One hot day, the caravan halted at a well with an old-fashioned windlass and bucket. For some reason, the procession moved off before Jeff, who was chained next to me, or myself had our drink. The bucket still had water in it when we came up to it. Instantly I seized it, took a half hitch on the chain, and held the bucket down for Jeff to drink. I heard the windlass rapidly unwinding back of us. Then there was a tightening of the rope and a crash, [and] trailing in the road back of us was what was left of the windlass and well casing.

Tossing the bucket aside, I went on my way without my drink, but with full contentment through the damage I had done. The slave dealer came down the line, but no one knew anything about the accident. This incident was bad for me because for the first time it came to me that I could get away with things and not be caught. That was the white man's brain at work in me.

There is just one more incident with Jeff and he passes from our picture forever. Late one hot afternoon, after a dragging day's walk, the caravan came to a stream, over which was a bridge, over which we could [have] gone with safety. But the slave trader for some reason, all his own, decided to put us through the stream by way of a ford. He did not know the ford but had the assurance that the water was low and the ford safe. Then he sent us in. Instead of striking the ford, the leader went below.

Everything went well until we reached the center of the stream, when without warning the leaders plunged into a hole. As the men ahead struggled through they pulled those back of them into the deep water. Fortunately, the hole was not wide, otherwise we would have been drowned. As it was, those behind held back, while those in front pulled ahead. Chained as we were together, we were pulled into the hole in spite of all our efforts to keep out of it. Desperately, we struggled, but the relentless chain dragged us on.

Seeing we were in for trouble, knowing Jeff was shorter than myself, I seized him as we went over the brink into the mass of struggling people. As I pushed Jeff up, I went down, the chain pulling me off my feet. I struggled to my knees only to be dragged flat on my face in the mud. We were dragged out unconscious. Jeff came to quickly, but it was some time before I recovered. As I look back, there it was, I first felt my ability to carry things through to a successful issue.

Don't forget that while I was young, I had [been] forced to take care of myself, so I was old in experience and quick at observation, different entirely from the crew to which I was hitched. Jeff went on his way but he taught me many things, through my service to him, because I hated the strong; not because I had any personal love for him.

Just a word about Alabama in the days of my journey. At that time we were in the midst of a forest cut by roads. Along the coast of the Gulf of Mexico, there were towns. But the interior was covered with a dense woods, which was being cleared as rapidly as possible for cotton fields. In the north, the clearing of a few acres was the task of years. The white pioneers took their time and did the job comfortably. Not so Alabama. Cotton was in demand, each field was a gold mine, so that Virginia, Kentucky, and Missouri, where cotton could not be raised, were the new breeding places for the slaves, who were sold south like their mules to clear away their forests.[2] Consequently the slaves were driven hard, early and late, to clearing the land for King Cotton. There was no letup in the driving. Forests were literally dragged out by the roots. It was into this situation that the men and women of our caravan were hurled, while the boys and girls were sent on into towns until they were stronger. For this reason, I was taken on to Mobile. There I was bought by a doctor, though I was a mere ragamuffin with a bad reputation. He was a gentleman of the Old South, kindhearted and very thoughtful of me. His treatment of me was all that I could hope for, so I responded to it and gave him no trouble, nor was I ever harshly treated by him.

There were two boys in the family, with whom I was soon on intimate terms. I knew so much more about the things of life they were always anxious to go hunting or fishing with me. On these excursions they taught me how to read and write. They also procured me books to read, which I read over and over again.

My education was carried on secretly; even the good doctor, who was truly my friend, did not know what was going on. Though there was a law, which was strictly enforced, against slaves being taught to read or write or have books, from that time forward, I always had several books at hand.[3] The boys were faithful in their task of supplying me with books from the home library, which was excellent. I read the Bible,

Shakespeare, and the English poets in the hayloft at odd times, when I was not driving the doctor to see his patients.

One morning all my world fell to ruin about my ears. It all came about through the doctor deciding to send my two boy friends to Yale.[4] At first it was planned that the boys should go alone. Then, much to my delight, the plans were changed and I was to go along as their servant, which pleased me greatly, because the boys had quietly promised me I could have all the books I could read. I was now 16, strong and sturdy. I had a complete new outfit, which pleased me greatly.

We went from Mobile to New Orleans by boat. From New Orleans, [we] went up the Mississippi by steamboat. Considering the emptiness of that big river of all river traffic at this time, you can't conceive of the varied and multitudes of river craft that fairly crowded it to its capacity at that time. You must remember the north was feeding the south, also clothing it, as well as supplying it with all sorts of manufactured articles. Steamboats, flatboats, keelboats, rafts, in fact anything that would float was loaded down with all sorts of stuff to be bartered and trafficked in every bayou and creek that reached the back door of the cotton planter.

For years before and even after the steamboat came, it was the custom of the farmers of Ohio and Indiana, as well as Pennsylvania, to put together a few timbers on which to load their plunder and float down the river to New Orleans, then dispose of their boats and walk back north, along the old Cherokee trail to the Ohio. Along the banks of this river were well-beaten trails, and taverns, to Cincinnati or Pittsburgh. At this time, the flatboatmen all took steamers to their destination.

Natchez-under-the-hill was at its height of wickedness and killings. It was like Dodge City in later days, when the cowboy, buffalo hunter, and bank robbers were in their zenith. Of course, Natchez was a source of attraction to my companions and myself. Even the good old doctor was interested in the sordidness and color of the most wicked city in America.[5] The shacks along the riverbank that sheltered the riffraff of the river was indescribably bad.

They were wood, one story high, low-browed and dirty. All flatboatmen were dressed alike in flowing red flannel shirts opened at the neck. With a broad-brimmed hat, a handkerchief tied loosely around their neck, a pair of jeans trousers stuffed down into the broad tops of rawhide boots, sleeves rolled up to their elbows, they were as rough a crew as could be found in any part of the world. Instead of pistols, they carried knives, which were more dependable at that time than firearms.

For some reason I never could fathom, there was an intense hatred between the raftsmen and flatboatmen. They went in gangs ready to pounce on each other at any turn of the street. In these fist battles, there was no limit placed on biting, clawing, kicking, hitting, or gouging of eyes. While no weapons were used, it was a combat of strength and brutality, maiming and killing its victims remorselessly.

The champion of the river at that time was a flatboatman [named] Mike Fink.[6] His fame was nationwide. His brutality towards men and women [was] beyond belief. Strange as it may seem, there was always some bully ready to challenge Mike at any big landing. Mike's reputed victims, gained by artfulness and strategy, were so colorful as to make good reading and plenty of talk wherever and whenever his name was mentioned.

The one story of that period about Mike which [I] remember was one about one of his numerous women. Mike, being suspicious of her loyalty, drove her ashore, tied her to a stake, piled up leaves and brush around her, set it afire, and left her to her fate. It was only the unexpected presence of a flatboatman that rescued the unfortunate woman that prevented her from being burned to death.

One more statement and I am through with the old days on the Mississippi. Every flatboat had in its crew either a bugler or a fiddler. It was the duty of these musicians to entertain both their own crew and announce their arrival at an evening landing, or approach to a large town. Some of these men became very proficient in their use of their instruments. Time and again [when] our steamer, the *Stag,* passed by a flatboat, the winding horn was blown in true English hunting style.[7] When they landed at night, when they cut loose in the morning, and all through the day, these blasts and fiddlings could be heard across the water.

Strange how silent and empty are the Ohio and Mississippi these days. All those crews of restless, sturdy, and rough strong men gone and mostly forgotten. I liked the river then much better than I do today.

At Pittsburgh, we left the river for the great and busy highway to Philadelphia. Like the rivers, the roads were filled with traffic going across the mountains for the west. Instead of flatboats, there were coaches, carriages, wagons, carts, everything that would . . . [run] on wheels were on the road. There were men who could handle six- and eight-horse teams with ease and expedition.

All drivers were known as wagoners, not teamsters as of today. They wore hobnailings and [were] ready to drink or fight whatever the occasion might require. Don't for a minute ever think that these pioneers were anything except what they were: rough, brutal, sturdy, and strong, with only their fists or a hobnailed boot to enforce their demands. A whole book could be written on the hobnailed boot as a weapon of offense and defense. The strategy of using a hobnail boot is an art; which had to be mastered if one took his place with the wagoners of the Allegheny Mountains. They too are gone, weapons, hobnailed boots, and men all faded out of the picture. So let them be.

At Philadelphia all my hopes and imaginations came to grief. It was this way. Quakers were the real abolitionists striving for the freedom of slaves.[8] This fact I was not aware of when I arrived in the city, but it was soon to be made known to me. While I was standing in front of our hotel, an elderly, dignified man passed me, looking intently at me, evidently endeavoring to attract my attention. Turning around, he came back, [and] looking around curiously, he whispered to me: "Look out tonight," then went on leaving me dazed. It all happened so suddenly I did not know what it was all about.

After thinking it over, I decided it was the two boys the stranger was giving me a warning about. Still undecided to take things in my own hands, to show my gratitude to the only people in the world who had shown any kindness to me . . . that night armed with a heavy soap dish as a weapon, I took up my watch at the door of the boys. I am afraid I was a poor watchman, for boylike, I soon went sound asleep.

Once I awakened, thought I heard mysterious and silent footsteps, then went sound asleep, to wake up in broad daylight. But when I went back to my room, there was a note on my pillow reading: "Be ready tonight." Now I knew I was the person involved. Just as soon as I could, I went to the good doctor with this note and told him of the incident of the previous day. He understood the significance of these messages, which put an end to my vicarious education at Yale. Without delay, I was taken to Baltimore, bidding my boy friends a heartbroken goodbye, while they went on to New Haven.

Upon our return to Mobile, the doctor very kindly advised me I would never make a house man. The other two openings were as a slave in the cotton fields or learn a trade. He advised me to take the latter course.[9] This matter decided, he apprenticed me to a white plasterer. Little did either of us know what this move meant to either of us. So ended my easy days and my contact with his library, which grieved me greatly. However, I had sense enough to know that the doctor was my friend, and was going a long, long way out of his way to serve me.

My apprenticeship was of short duration. While I was willing, the man was a drunkard and began abusing me on the very first day. Being apt and observing, I soon could do rough jobs. Setting me to a task which I knew was beyond my ability, I did the best I could. The plasterer when he saw my work flew into a rage, [and] beat me with a lath with a nail in it, until I had to go to a hospital for slaves. It was kept by a white woman who was inexperienced, and a heartless creature, as she not only neglected her patients, but would beat them unmercifully at the least provocation.

I stood by helplessly and watched her beat the helpless. She was beating a woman with a rawhide whip when I protested. Instantly, [she] struck me across the face. Without a thought of what I was doing, I seized the whip and gave the white woman a sound beating, then ran out of the house, knowing full well what would happen to me if I was caught. All day long I hid in the piles of freight on the New Orleans boat dock, determined I would take the boat that night. I had been to New Orleans, knew my way about; that was as far as I could think. One thing I did know: I had to get out of Mobile. Even the good doctor could not protect me. Without bidding my kind friend the doctor goodbye, I stole on board the New Orleans steamer, and launched myself on an adventure that carried [me] into strange places and stranger incidents.

TWO

ALL NIGHT LONG I was in a state of apprehension. I knew at New Orleans the steamer would be met by officers of the law who would take note of every person who came off the boat the next morning. The law and society were organized to catch any misguided wretch who thought he could slip through the net spread for him. I had committed an unforgivable crime, and I was well aware of it. I had made up my mind I would get off the boat safely or else go to the river for my final escape from a life that had already become intolerable to me.

It was a drippy and wet morning when the steamer docked in broad daylight at New Orleans. I boldly went forward among the passengers who were grouped in the bow ready to go ashore. From this position I picked out the officers whom I was to elude. There they stood at the foot of the gangplank ready to leap onto poor deluded me. As I stood wondering without a plan, I happened to see the kitchen supplies piled up on the dock.

Without waiting for the last passenger to go ashore, I leaped upon the plank, ran down with alacrity and seized a bag of potatoes, and waited with a quaking heart. My boldness evidently deceived the officers as they stood silently by, giving me no further attention.

When the last passenger was ashore, I picked up the bag of potatoes and trotted aboard, carrying them to the kitchen. There the cook thought I was a boy from ashore. By the time I had made a few trips with the provisions, no one thought of asking me to give an account of myself. After begging breakfast from the cook, I walked confidently down the gangplank, past the officers, and across the quay as though I had a perfect right to do so.

As there were a number of lads of my own age and color on the streets of the city, as long as I kept walking, I knew no one would question my presence. At noontime I realized what was going to menace my safety. It was food. I dare not beg, I could not ask for work, I had no money, but I must eat. I walked the streets all day, plagued by an appetite that dogged me as I walked. My hope was [that] under cover of night, I could steal. Even then I was under restraint, because there was a curfew hour, past which I did not dare be on the street.

Rather than take chances, I went to bed early on top of a pile of cotton covered with a tarpaulin. Cotton in the fluff is soft enough for a bed, but in the bale it is hard and ungiving, so I slept restlessly. It may seem strange that I am able to give all these minor details of my wanderings, but impressions of that period were indelible and marked on my mind, which is [a] pretty good one, if I am compelled to give this evidence myself.

Broad daylight is no time for a runaway slave to crawl out from beneath a tarpaulin on the docks of New Orleans. Several times I endeavored to get out from under the covering, but neighboring voices were too menacing for me to take chances. By noon my hunger and my fears drove me to desperation. As I had not eaten anything since the morning before, I was in such a frame of mind I did not care what happened. Fearfully, I pushed the heavy tarpaulin aside and stepped out into the sunshine, which fairly blinded me by its brightness. I stood dazed for a moment, expecting to be pounced upon, but my good fortune was with me. Much to my delight I stepped off as sprightly as if I had an important matter in the city.

Wandering farther and farther away from the dock, my hunger fairly over came me. So I went back and walked along the river determined to find food or make my last leap into the river for my freedom. Again I was disappointed. Resolutely, I set my face towards the city. As I came out on a side street from the dock, I came onto a large frame house standing all alone in a well-dressed yard of grass.

This house had a personality of friendliness, at least I thought it had at the time, which invited me to come in. I needed no second invitation to enter. Boldly I walked up to the back door, opened it, and entered without knocking.

I walked straight into paradise, for there on the stove was a pot of beans, spreading its beneficent fragrance on the empty air. Not exactly empty either, for there was an old Negro cook occupying her part of the air. Her presence played no part in my life just then. It was the odor of the bean soup that overwhelmed me. There was no fooling that cook. She took one short look at me. My heart sank low down, and I thought it was all over with me. But she was a wise and friendly soul who knew. Without either of us saying a word, she went to the cupboard, took out a good-sized bowl, put it in front of me, handed me a ladle, pointed at the pot of soup, and went out of the room.

The astounding fact remains that all the years that have passed have not completely blotted out the taste of that soup. I fairly oozed bean soup when I had finished [feeding] the gnawing of a demanding stomach. I waited for my friend to come back, but she never did. I am sure, however, that I heard the slats of the window shutter rattle as I walked slowly by them on my way [out]. With a full [stomach], life took on a new aspect as I left behind me that friendly house and the kindly old cook, and the fragrant bean pot.

There was a fascination about the river that I could not resist, because I knew that was my only avenue of escape from my bondage, which grew more and more hateful to me. As I sauntered along the dock, I came on a steamer which was being loaded with freight. Looking up, I saw a large sign: "For Memphis and Upriver Points."

Out of a clear blue sky there came to me as clearly as though some one had spoken it aloud: "That's your boat." Furthermore it was to leave that night. I had not the least doubt from that time forward I would be safely aboard when she cast off on her trip north. That decision having been made, I went back to the city as contented as though I was to be a first-class passenger instead of a stowaway.

As soon as it was good and dark I went back to my steamer, the *Magnolia*.[10] It was one thing, I discovered, to receive a message from the high heavens, but it was quite another thing to fulfill that message. When I came back to take my steamer, the dock was alive with stevedores loading the boat, besides the usual spectators who gather to see a steamer start on its way to places they would like to go. They were all there; so was I with all eyes to see what could be done for myself.

Great iron baskets swinging on iron rods, filled with resin, lighted up the scene, much to my confusion. I mention all these as being of a personal nature to me, because they were my active friends or enemies. If you have never seen one of these old-time fire baskets in operation, you have no idea how brightly a puddle of resin thrown on the fire will illuminate a wide area. The one compensation to me about my glowing enemy, the fire basket, was that [after] a brief moment of intense brilliance, then it began to fade away until it threatened to go out completely. It was a fitful and unsatisfactory light, but it was the best that could be had and held full sway on the river up to the time of the coming of electric lights—quite a space of time.

Standing in the shadow of a pile of cotton, I watched and watched and wondered and wondered how I was to get aboard my steamer. The blazing fire pots [were] at both ends of the gangplank on which the deck hands walked back and forth. There were cables that tied the steamer to the dock, but I was no tightrope walker, so they were dismissed. There apparently was no means left for one except [to] go up that broad gangplank. If that was my way, it was my way, was my fatalistic conclusion.

Just as I was about to take my fate in my own hands, my way opened up. It was in a narrow gangplank in the bow which the deckhands threw out when they tied up the forward cables. I saw how plainly it was lighted up when the fire box blazed and how much it was in the dark when it faded away. What further gladdened my heart was, there was an open hatch at the end of the board that led to the hull. My lucky star I felt was shining as I made my way toward the dock end of the slim and narrow board. When the light in the fire box faded out, I made a run for it, dropped into the hold, just as my enemy the fire box lighted even the hold where I was lying panting with fear. But then I was unseen, safely aboard my steamer bound north. This episode I believe gave me confidence in myself, in my ability to meet any and all situations which might arise to confront me.

Now that I was in the hold it was easy for me to disappear into the black void that surrounded me. The next thing was to find a safe hiding place, to which I might retire in case of a necessity. Then came my first surprise, for I found absolutely nothing in the hold except a few bales of cotton. It never occurred to me until it was forced upon me now that river steamers carried no cargo in their holds. As a matter of fact, the hull was merely a floating platform, on which a superstructure of deck and cabin were built. The cargo was carried openly on deck. At the time, this did not mean a thing to my enthusiastic, youthful soul.

Climbing on top of a bale of cotton, I went sound asleep through sheer exhaustion. Waking up and feeling the vibration of the boat, I felt happy indeed that I was on my way to freedom. A sniff of the bilgewater told me a fearful story. Making my way forward, I found the latch fastened down. It was so high overhead I could not reach it. I hastened back to the stern to find the aft latch fastened as well. I was a prisoner in the hold with nothing to eat or drink. The foul air and solid blackness did not help the situation. I went back to my cotton bale, sat on top of it, and had a good think.

Matters did not straighten themselves out to my liking. All I could see then was starvation ahead of me, because the latches would not be taken off until Memphis, which meant several days. However, I lay down and went to sleep. When I woke up, I was festered with thirst more than hunger. I tried to drink the bilgewater, but it made me deathly sick. Then I took to wandering aimlessly around in the darkness hoping to find something, I did not know what. Then I went to sleep on my friendly bale of cotton.

Waking moments were filled with anguish of thirst and hunger. The steamer stopped several times, taking on and putting off freight. At such times, the hold was perfectly quiet, so I felt if the worst came to worst I could pound on the hatch and be heard. My trouble was that the hull was so deep, I could not reach the latch.

My only chance was to roll my bale of cotton up near the hatch. By clambering on top of it I could hammer on the hatch with my fists. How much time I was at this task [I do not know], but after much exertion I finally succeeded in getting it almost to the hatch. By this time my thirst was almost unendurable. Weaving around and around in the darkness, I suddenly felt a drop of moisture strike my hand. I stopped [and] held my breath, lest the least movement of mine would take me away from this precious gift. I waited when again there came that slow drop. Holding my hand steady, I moved my body until it had taken the position of my hand, then stood with my mouth wide open to receive that welcome drop. It never came again.

THREE

FORTUNATELY FOR ME, I was not strong enough to move my bale of cotton or I would have been caught as I lay on top of my bale [of] cotton dead to the world. It seemed like a dream when I felt fresh air and the sunshine streaming down into the hold. Sitting up, I saw it all coming to my rescue, as there was a ladder going straight up through the hatch to the deck.

You may call it crazy luck, but when I dragged myself up on deck there was not a soul in sight except the deckhands, who were eating their evening meal. One of the men, catching sight of me, never said a word but took the plate of food of the man next to him, emptied it into his own, gave me his cup of coffee, and motioned me to go back into the hold. I shook my head. Pouring out most of the coffee, he handed me what was left. This I gulped down ravenously. Now that I felt somewhat stronger, I felt differently about giving myself up. As I had not been seen by any of the officers of the steamer, I decided to trust myself to the recesses of the black hole. As I went down the ladder, the deckhand who had befriended me handed me another cup of coffee.

My fascination for this shaft of fresh air and sunshine proved to be my undoing. I had hardly seated myself at the foot of the ladder when a shadow was thrown across my plate. Looking up, I stared into the glaring face of an angry white mate, who commanded me to come on deck. If I had given my situation a second thought, I would have answered his command. Instead, I cast my plate aside and disappeared in[to] the darkness of the hold, holding tightly to my cup of coffee. The mate hurried down the ladder, shouting as he came. The louder he swore, the faster I ran, until I reached my bales of cotton. Fortunately for me, most of my coffee was gone. What was left I drank with great relish. My situation was serious, but what could I do about it, until the hunt started?

My wait was all too short. For the search for me began as soon as the mate could get his men into the hold. He was afraid to trust his men with a lighted lantern for fear they would accidentally set the steamer afire. All he could do was to make his men catch hold of [their] hands and feel their way along in their drive. I lay down flat on my face on the floor. By the time the chain of hunters, stretching from one side of the hull to the other, advanced slowly but surely to where I was stretched out. I could hear the men breathing heavily in the darkness but could not place them until one stepped on my leg. The man never faltered, but calmly [went] on with his comrades. I knew my escape from the trap was only temporary, for when the men had gone from stem to stern in their fruitless search, the mate accused them of letting me slip through their line. Ordering the men to stand still, he called for another mate to bring down two lighted lanterns.

A second line was formed with the two officers with lighted lanterns following close behind. Then I knew my case was hopeless. I crawled as close as I could to the bales of cotton and stood in their shadow. As the lights closed in about me, I saw the lone coffee tin cup. Reaching down, I picked it up as the nearest lantern came close to me. I hurled the tin cup at the light but missed it.

In another moment, two strong arms were around me, and the manhunt was at an end. As soon as I was captured, I collapsed and was carried on deck in this helpless condition. My cries for food and drink attracted the attention of a woman passenger, who, forcing her way through the crowd surrounding me, took possession of me. She had me taken to her own cabin, where she . . . gave me food and water until I was out of danger.

By the second day I had so far recovered, the captain of the steamer began to question me, endeavoring to make me tell where I came from. He knew I was a runaway, [and] his duty was to take me back to my master. But I refused to give him any information. Failing in his inquiry, he informed me he would leave me with the sheriff at the next landing, picking me up on his way back to New Orleans. I learned I was somewhere between Vicksburg and Memphis. Sure enough, the captain at the next stop placed me in custody of the sheriff for safekeeping.

As we were going through the little town, the proprietor of a grocery store asked about me, but the sheriff explained I was a runaway and he was taking me to jail for safekeeping. The grocery [man] suggested that instead of locking me up, the thing for the sheriff to do was to [use me as] help in clearing off the officer's farm. This advice, much to my surprise, was accepted. So instead of going to jail, I was sent out into the country to work in the open air. Though the work was hard, I was a willing worker, for I was already casting about to find some way to escape.

Gaining my freedom by hook or crook was never out of my mind. Knowing the steamer was expected back shortly, I began my calculations as to the time of her arrival. The sheriff proved to be a better index than I was. For one afternoon seeing him in close conference with his overseer, and noticing they glanced at me slyly from time to time, I made up my mind that it was high time for me to go on my way.

When the sheriff left, the overseer kept close tabs on every movement I made. I knew I had to outwit him or be an unwilling passenger on the steamer to New Orleans. Keeping a close watch on the foreman, I began to be very busy in a fence corner filled with stubborn brush. Bending low over my work, I managed to loosen a lower rail in the fence. When the overseer turned his back, I was down on all fours clearing and digging my way under and through that loose rail.

Once out on the other side, bending low, I ran towards a swamp which was in plain view. Soon the ground was soft and underbrush so thick I was afraid I would be captured before I could get into the refuge of the swamp. I plunged ahead, the ground getting softer and the underbrush thinner and thinner until I came to [a] sluggish pool, sour and soft. My feet sunk into the slime and mud so deep it looked for a time as though I would be swallowed up.

I managed to get loose, and clinging to a log that almost reached the other side of the pool, I determined to risk a leap into the muck on the other side. I lighted fairly in the midst of the quagmire and if I had not thrown myself forward on my face and dragged myself across the hole like an alligator, I would be there yet.

As it was, I was completely exhausted when I sunk down on a clump of bushes that held me aloft until I caught my breath. Making my way along half-buried logs and bushes, I kept getting deeper and deeper into the swamp, until I came to a clump of four trees with intertwining roots, making a small elevation rising above the soggy ground. As it was almost dark, I made up my mind I would stay here for the night.

These four forest friends rose straight out of the swamp,

with matted branches stretching overhead like a huge umbrella. Knowing the forest was full of wolves and catamounts, in dim twilight I broke down a branch, making a club for my defense. I climbed up into the forks of one of the trees just like Robinson Crusoe, the first night he was ashore on his island, but I was afraid I would go to sleep and fall. Wet, tired, and hungry, I sat down with my back against the trunk of the tree, determined to spend the night on guard. But I was soon sound asleep. Being awakened by a hoot owl— that gave me a great scare.

When I was shivering and staring fearfully about me, I heard the yelping of hounds, the despair of fugitive slaves. The sound grew louder and louder, closer and closer, until the pack went howling by me. Then I knew it was wolves chasing a deer. Then I saw in my imagination a catamount crouching overhead ready to spring down on me, which I soon saw was only a gnarled knot. Relieved of this terror, I refused to believe my eyes or ears and went sound asleep, leaving the forest and the swamp to take care of themselves.

In the morning I slid off my tree island in the opposite direction from which I had come on it the night before. For a time, the going was bad, very bad. Then it got better. In the middle of the morning, I found a patch of blueberries. They satisfied my hunger and quenched my thirst, so I was quite ready to go on. The strange part of this dreary swamp was the absence of life. Of course there were plenty of ugly and dreaded water moccasins. There was not a bird to be seen, or even a rabbit. Everything decent seemed to pass by this bit of forsaken land.

About noon, I struck a road which led me to a broad green savannah, where the ground was firm and luscious grass [was] up to my knees. What was best of all, overhead the sun was still shining. As I was gathering blueberries close to a fallen log, I happened to look up and saw a large body of water.

Then I knew I was back on the banks of the Mississippi. There was a large steamer coming downstream. To make my story dramatic it should have been the *Magnolia,* but unfortunately it was some other steamer whose name meant nothing to me. I stood on the bank and watched the steamer sail majestically by, for I want to say right now, there was something proud and majestic the way a large river steamer swam the waters. They were a sight never to be forgotten.

While I was silently watching the steamer go by, my meditations were brought to an abrupt end, by seeing a colored woman bending over her washtub. At the same time I saw a skiff pulled up on shore a short distance below her. At the sight of the skiff I forgot the presence of the washer woman, and made straight past her for the skiff. It was only the work of a moment to push the skiff out into the stream. Every moment I expect the colored woman to let forth a disturbing yell, but she went about her work as though nothing had happened. Having bathed my face and eaten a lunch which I found in the skiff, I felt ready for new adventures.

My liberty threatened to be short-lived, for as I was rowing along, a white man with a shotgun sprang out of the bushes, ordering me to come ashore. As I paid no attention to him, he rushed down to the water's edge, pointing his gun at me, threatening to shoot. I knew that a dead fugitive slave was of no value to him.[11] I rowed along shore just out of his reach, until I had the man worked up into such a crazy frenzy I was afraid he might shoot me. Turning the bow of my boat to the middle of the river, I went on down the river.

Events moved rapidly after this adventure with the man and his shotgun. I had barely gone downstream a couple of miles until I saw a skiff with two men coming out from shore ahead of me. Then I knew I was in for trouble. I could not turn around and go upstream. My only chance was to beat them to the other shore. The race was on with all the advantage to my opponents. Though I rowed at top speed, the men gained on me rapidly. Though they caught up with me and called on me to give up, I had no intention of doing so until I was overpowered. Seeing my game, they spurted ahead, drove their boat across my bow.

I smashed right into them on a theory as long as I was free something might happen to give me a last chance. But my theory went wrong, for I had hardly struck them when my boat was grabbed, and before I could strike them with my oar, they were on me, [and] my game for the present was lost. Before I had realized what had happened, I was lying in the bottom of my captors' boat with my arms tied tightly behind me. I expected no favors from these men, as to them I was only a beast of labor in revolt—which was perfectly true.

The two men pushed and hauled me up the bank to their log cabin, all the while plying me with questions, which I refused to answer. They then informed me they would take me to town the next day, which I knew meant my old friend the sheriff, from whom I had just escaped, would clap me into jail. In the meantime, I was to make myself comfortable in the back room of their cabin.

It took some pleading on my part to get them to loosen my hands, which they finally did. Left alone, I took notice of my surroundings. I was in a small log-house room with no opening in it except a rude door which opened into the front room. A bundle of dirty rags in a corner was to be my bed and a cracker box on end my chair; otherwise there was not another thing in that den.

As I passed through the front room, I saw a man evidently very ill lying helpless in his bunk. As I was shoved into my prison room, one of the men pointed to the pile of rags in the corner jestingly, told me a man had just died there, so I might be disturbed by ghosts.

When my evening meal of cornbread and fat meat swimming in grease was pushed through a crack in the door, I was informed that my escape was impossible, as boxes were going to be piled against the door. Furthermore, if I got by them, the big dog in the yard would finish me up in short order. This I believed, as I had noticed the vicious brute as I passed through the yard coming in. I heard the boxes piled up against the door, which seemed a good burglar alarm to me, and to be reckoned with when I made my effort to escape. I had no intention of staying put in that cabin overnight. Knowing of the barricade and of the dog only made me the more determined to get away.

From time to time during the evening I could hear my captors moving about, and I am sure [I] heard them . . . stand quietly at my door, listening to find out what I was doing. I sat in silence on the cracker box just as actively planning to get away as they were to hold me.

It was late when I took off my shoes, tied them together, and made ready to escape. I could hear the deep breathing of the two men. I had no fears of an outbreak from the sick man. Satisfied I could begin work, I put my weight gently against the door, but it held fast. Sure of my plan, I put more pressure on the door, but it would not move.

Perhaps they had put a bar across the door. That thought made me feel queer. Determined to test that fact, I put my whole weight against that door, care what would. To my relief, it gave a trifle. Then I knew I would surely get by that barrier. Patiently and slowly I pushed the pile of boxes inch by inch until I could squeeze through. The two men were sound asleep as I, with thieflike silence, stole into the front room.

The sick man on whom I had not counted now proved to be a disturbing menace. For he had heard me, [and] thinking it was one of his companions, he asked me for a drink. I had seen the water bucket on a bench at the side of the door. Holding my breath, I walked quietly to the door, stepped out into the moonlight, and jostled a gourd dipper against the bucket, thus indicating the bucket was empty.

Picking up the water bucket, I started toward the gate. That dog came from somewhere that I did not stop to see, as he stood squarely across my path, growling as though he meant business. I pushed that water bucket into his muzzle and walked on as though I was going to the spring. My boldness bluffed that dog into silence, while he was still suspicious and followed me. Having followed me to the last fence corner, he stood watching me as I disappeared still swinging that water bucket, all the time fearful that he would let out a yowl that would raise [the men and] put an end to my easy walkaway.

Now being left to myself, I threw the bucket away and ran across lots down to the river. Knowing that I would be followed by the lads, I waded up the river. Coming to a small creek, I followed that until I came to a ford. There I went ashore, as my footprints would be mingled with those of the people who had gone before me.

At daylight, I made my way to the riverbank and hid in a clump of willows. Sometime in the afternoon, I noticed three flatboats tied together being worked ashore by the men at the long sweeps, evidently making a landing. I had been watching them come down the river, wondering what they were trying to do, so my curiosity was aroused by one of the men leaping ashore just below where I was hiding, take a half turn around a tree, [and] paying out his rope until the boat swung quietly against the bank. Now what were they up to? As the three men threw out a slim plank, and came down it with their axes, I knew they were going to "wood up." I watched them cut up the driftwood and carry it aboard for some time, before I saw a way out for me.

Stealing out of the willows, I made my way to the top of

the bank coming out just above the boats. I stood watching the boatmen, as though I belonged to a neighboring plantation. Then I went down the bank offering my assistance. The men hesitated, but when I admitted I lived nearby, they gladly accepted my services. After the first trip or so, the men paid no further attention to me. But I was all eyes for my own opportunities. The wood was being piled against the three shanty houses. They were small affairs with no places of concealment.

But the cargo which consisted of hogsheads of tobacco were the very places I was looking for. The hogsheads were stacked upon end and not too close together. Though the boats were headed down the river, I knew I had to get out of the country and this was my one great chance.

As I took on a load of wood, I would leisurely go to the outside boat and stand looking idly up and down the river, making no haste to go back to shore. On shore I could loaf among the trees. The result was the men gave little heed to me, except to call me a "lazy nigger." They were too busy to watch me. Keeping a close watch on the boatman, I took a load of wood to the shanty in the outside boat, then when no one was looking dropped down into the hold.

Like a rat I had disappeared into a hiding place of quick choosing, poor it was, but I had to take a chance. There I lay with quick ears to catch the alarm of my disappearance. Casting off I heard the boatmen walking back and forth as they lazily plied their long heavy sweeps, in order to get out into the current of the river, which was their motive power. It was dark when a watchman put up his red and green signal lanterns on the bow of the flatboat. I was lying immediately beneath him. It seemed to me, right out in the open, all he had to do was to glance down and I would be discovered. My good fortune again stood me in stead while he went whistling back to the shanty.

FOUR

IT WAS PITCH dark when I clambered out of my uncomfortable hiding place. At first I was quite cautious lest I be discovered. But being satisfied the boatmen were all asleep, I decided to stretch my legs, by crawling over the hogsheads to a better hiding place. I grew too venturesome, and the first thing I knew a heavy hand held me fast by the collar. It was the night watchman, who had been watching me like a cat does a mouse as it steals from its hole. After tiring of playing with my stealthiness, he leaped onto me. There was no denying I was his victim, for he gripped both my wrists until I could not raise my arms, and pushed me ahead of him so I could not use my feet or I would have kicked him into the river and gone after him.

Helpless as I was, he pushed me to the shanty, kicked open the door, and yelled, "The lazy nigger's aboard." In less time than I am telling you, the other man, by the name of Joe, was on his feet blinking at me by the poor light of a lantern.

To properly understand the positions that these men were placed in, by my hiding aboard their crafts, you must go back to the time of which I am speaking. I was worth $1,800. For one to run away meant a loss of that much money, and anyone who aided me was a thief, worse than a thief, because he was an enemy to the institution of slavery. So the hand of the law, the anger of the people, and the consolidated fear of the south were all in a hot cry after anyone who helped to break down their institutions. The penalties were severe—not only sending the rescuer to jail but confiscating his property as well. In this instance, the flatboats and the tobacco would all have been taken, though their owners had neither aided me nor concealed me. In addition to this vengeance of the law, the flatboat[men] were a rough ugly crew, which meant rough going for me.

I was hustled to the shanty of the middle boat. There a rough giant of a man called Tom was aroused. He was red-headed and red-bearded. Neither seemed to have known the touch of a comb for some time past. I knew his type as soon as I saw him. You see, I had been on this river on my way to New Haven, so I was familiar with the people who lived along it, also those who lived on it. Tom was a bully, a river bully with a reputation for cruelty and meanness, which he no doubt enjoyed. The captains of the other two boats were Bill and Joe. It was easy to see that Tom was their boss.

I had to make a quick estimate of them, so I could play my part, and get them on my side, which was a poor one, any way you looked at it. Bill was a fat blubbery body, slow of thought, and slower in action. Joe was short, thin, with a monkey face, and about as much intelligence. These were my judges. Big Tom blinked and swore at me. Three stools were drawn up to a rough table in which sat a smoky lantern, as they sat down to talk it over.

I soon saw that neither of them held the least sympathy for me. The only thing in their minds was how to get rid of me quickly and finally. Tom made no bones about his plan, which was to kill me. All agreed this was desirable. But now, all

Tom asked was for Bill and Joe to get out and leave me in his care.

Pressed as to his method of execution, he coldly put into words his evil intent, [which] was to strangle me and throw me overboard. To this both men assented, until Joe raised the question that my body would rise to trouble them. Then greasy, fat Bill suggested the cat method for my extermination by way of a heavy weight tied around my neck. This seemed to satisfy Joe's objection, so they set about to carry out their plan.

As I sat at the head of the table, the gloom of the shanty was nothing compared to that which enveloped me. All my fatalism disappeared in a fear that paralyzed me, body and mind. To sit and listen there to this macabre dance of death, and see the big ogrelike hands of Tom, as he worked them back and forth, itching to strangle me, scared me helplessly. All of my courage oozed out like the quicksilver in a broken thermometer. I was a[n] inert mass, without a being.

Once the plan of my execution having been determined, they were all too quick to carry it into effect. First they tied my hands behind me. There were ample stones at hand in the fireplace. There was a tigerish gleam in Tom's eyes as he lifted a large stone and dropped it onto the table in front of me, [making a noise] that echoed through that dimly lighted death chamber, like a ghostly knell of doom. I sat silently and dumb in the ghastly scene.

Everything went on schedule until Tom fastened the rope around my neck, at the other end of which was the stone. Then, Joe weakened and refused to go on. All that I remember of the conversation in this whole affair was what Tom said now: "Every damn cent I have in the world is in this boat, and I'm not going to lose it for a lazy worthless nigger."

Little Joe was afraid from another cause. So far as his conscience was concerned, he made it plain [it] did not bother him. What did bother him was the presence of the other flat-boats, any one of whom might betray him. An altercation arose among the three immediately. Tom and Bill were determined to throw me overboard and take their chances. Joe was unmovable. The row started when Bill started to tie the rope around my neck. There was a weapon at hand, which had I known of its presence, I feel I would have used.

Joe reached out in the gloom and brought forth an ax; at the same time, he pulled me to my feet, pushing me ahead of him. He swung the ax in front of him. With one blow he beat down the shanty door. The cool air and open sky, even though my hands were tied behind me, seemed like freedom to me, at least it gave me heart to think. Joe pulled me across the boats to his shanty and closed the door behind us with a bang. He was at the rope holding my hand, immediately, loosening it so that I was an able-bodied man again.

Tom and Bill, still determined to have me, came and stood by Joe's door, as they argued with him to deliver me into their hands. Joe with ax in hand stood inside the door, ready for action, listening but stubbornly refused to give me up. Tom and Bill retired to their shanty. There were two dull thuds. Joe threw open the door and I saw Tom with an ax in hand, as our boat swung clear of the other two boats. He had cut the rope tying the boats together.

As they could not dispose of me, they trapped Joe by sending him adrift with me on board. It was now up to Joe to get rid of me. It was my plan that Joe adopted to effect this purpose. Remembering how the pirates made their victims walk the plank, I now suggested that he and his helper, running the boat close to shore, run out the plank and let me run and jump off the end. This Joe agreed to do. Before walking the plank, I begged Joe to give me something to eat.

He proved to be kindly enough now that he was on his own. [He] let me build a fire and cook all the ham and eggs I could eat. This meal over, I made ready to go. Joe and his man had the boat close to shore. The landing plank was in position. There was no ceremony in my leaving. Dropping the end of his sweep, he ran the plank out as far as it would go and be safe for him. With a word of gratitude, I ran and jumped and went down over my head. As I could swim, a few strokes and I was ashore. I yelled a goodbye to Joe, but he was too glad to get rid of me forever to answer.

FIVE

It DIDN'T TAKE me long to find out that I had landed in a canebreak, which was impenetrable. I was too exhausted to do anything but go into the cane, lie down, and forget my troubles in a deep sleep. The sun was high when I woke up. Last night was a terrible nightmare but my wet clothes were ample evidence of its realities. With the river on one side and the impenetrable canebrake on the other, I had no alternative but to follow the . . . [worn] river bench either up- or down-stream. For some unknown reason, I decided to go down-stream. After walking for some time, I came to a road leading back into the country, which was a relief from the uncertain sand of the river shore.

I was in a country where the slaves had their freedom to go and come in daylight, so I boldly struck down the road, depending upon my own resourcefulness. I ran into a party of slaves without warning. Asking for a drink of water, I was directed to the house just ahead. With this . . . [information], I waited until they had disappeared, then took the woods skirting the fields of the house, which was in plain sight, coming back to the road beyond.

Everything went well with me until the middle of the afternoon. I came to a blacksmith's shop at a crossroad. After careful scouting, finding the smith was a colored man, I decided to go boldly to him asking for both water and food. I could see he knew who I was, as he directed me to the water bucket at the other end of the shop. I had hardly finished drinking when a white man rode up to the other side of the shop and asked of the smith if he had seen a runaway.

If I had used my head, I would have known he was looking for someone else besides me. Instead, I started on a dead run out of the shop. My suspicious action brought the man at my heel. Knowing he was mounted, I made for a fence and ran across the fields towards a group of slaves at work. As I came close to the field hands, I saw a young woman, who I instinctively knew would protect me.

She saw the man on horseback chasing me, so I needed no introduction. Grabbing a large basket used for holding cotton, she motioned me to climb into it. She then threw several gunny bags over me. My pursuer evidently knew of my hiding place, for he came directly to the young woman, asked her if she had seen me. He was very crafty in his method of approach, for before I knew what was going on, he had upset the basket, and I was thrown sprawling on the ground.

My judgment of the woman was correct, for before the man could seize me the woman was on him like a wild beast. The last I saw of her she was fighting, scratching, holding her man, like I was one of her own children. I have often wondered what happened to her, for she certainly was in for a severe whipping.

Once away from the fields across which I ran like a scared rabbit, I hid in my friend the forest until night. Now I had to watch my steps closely, for a slave abroad at night was always examined closely. Whither I was going I did not know, but wherever it was I determined not to stand still in a county on the lookout for a fugitive slave. Gaining the road, I walked until I came to a large town, which proved to be Vicksburg.

Once in the streets, as it was still early, I was safe. Making for the river, I found a steamer taking on cotton. The flaring fire boxes were my enemies, but the water was deep, as the stern of the boat was snug against the bank. I had no trouble leaping aboard in the dark. I ran into a colored deckhand, who hid me on top of bales of cotton. When he told me the steamer was bound for New Orleans, for once I thought my lucky star had failed me. I made up my mind anyplace was preferable to Vicksburg just now, [and] I stowed away hoping for the best.

The steamer had hardly gotten under way when the Negro who had hid me brought a white mate to my hiding place, the only time I was ever betrayed by one of my own color. [12] Knowing I could not escape, I climbed down at the first command of the mate, quietly giving myself up. This time I was shackled on the lower deck where I was in plain view. I made no effort to escape. In sheer despair, I resigned myself to my fate.

At New Orleans I was taken to jail and locked up in a cell. Every effort was made to learn from me where I came from and the name of my master. Having made up my mind it was better for me to face the unknown than to go back to Mobile and face the known, I stubbornly refused to give any information about myself. I noticed immediately that this attitude rather pleased the officials—why, I was able to discover later.

From the very first I made myself agreeable and ingratiated myself with my jailer. The police soon let me out of my cell, so I had the run of the jail. I had made up my mind there was no use of breaking jail like a ragamuffin. I had to be well dressed to walk the streets of New Orleans. I could have escaped at any time I pleased.

For ten months I educated myself how to outwit men and combinations. During this period I worked out a method which gave me a great advantage in meeting situations that arose in the future. Mind you, I was dealing with ignorant men. I soon saw that they were slow thinkers, that they did absolutely nothing more than they were compelled to do, that they were always putting themselves on the blind side of any movement.

Being of an active mind, I occupied myself by working out imaginary plans of escape. For the ten months I was in jail, I worked out these problems until formulating certain theories which were of great use to me later on. For instance, I soon demonstrated that a man with a plan always had the advantage of an unsuspecting person. Second, timing of execution was even more important than a plan.

There were certain positions which were blind spots to my captors. If I occupied one of these blind spots, if I timed my next movement correctly, I could do anything up to murder without my victim knowing of my presence. It became a sort of a play with me, which I enjoyed, because I made the white man helpless against me.

Another advantage over my white adversaries was that I knew I was an animal worth $2,000. I knew that there was some game on that would give someone besides my owner $2,000. In order to cash in I had to be dressed up and sold on the auction block. I was merely waiting patiently for that time to come. In the meantime, I read all the newspapers I could get, by using the simple ruse of tearing them in two pieces, throwing them around until I could be alone, when I would put them back together again.

In this way, I learned the auction days, how many slaves were sold, and where they came from. I found the greater number came down the river from Kentucky and Missouri, that the steamers arrived early in the morning. With this information I was ready. But as I have said it was ten months before the cashing-in move was made.

One morning I was taken from jail downtown completely fitted out in new wearing apparel from a new hat to new shoes. Everything was of the best, so I knew I was to be sold as a house boy. If I do say it myself I was very much better dressed and more intelligent-looking than the white men, which pleased my vanity and modified my anger against my inveterate and hated enemies.

From the clothing store I was taken to the slave pen for inspection and sale. I made up my mind I was going to select my owner, so when anyone came to inspect me I did not like, I answered all questions with a "yes" and made myself disagreeable. So far as I was concerned, the game was on and I began to play it.

Having the freedom of the place, I set out to get my data for a plan of escape. I soon saw that there was a large gate through which the caravan of slaves entered into the pen. This gate was heavy and was opened inward by an old man very slowly. In the process of opening he had his back to the entrance.

I recognized the blind spot of my plan. My next move was the timing of my plan. I soon discovered that if I stood at a certain spot, I could not be seen by anyone in the pen. That was my timing spot. Boldly played, I knew I could beat the existing combination, particularly with my new suit of clothes.

I knew the next day was auction day, [and] I would be put on the block. Knowing that the slaves from upriver would enter that gate that morning, I was ready and waiting to execute my plan. At the appointed time the old man opened the gate, with his back to me. In an instant I stepped off my blind spot making for the gate as the slaves came through, thereby intervening their bodies between me and the gate man. It was so easy it seemed impossible. But then I was outside of the pen on a wide-open street.

Instead of walking briskly away, I was shrewd enough to stand idly by and watch the cavalcade go through, then, timing myself, I moved away slowly, keeping close to the fence, which increased the blind spot of the gate man, so that when he did see me, I was so far away, if he saw me at all, he was convinced I could not have gotten through the entrance and be that distance away. I was free once more and on my own.

That Mississippi River attracted me like a magnet, for as soon as I was free to move in my own selected direction I made straight for the river. My good clothes was my open sesame, for I was not even noticed as I strolled by steamer after steamer. Coming to barrels of flour, up on end, I carelessly sat on top of one, to think over my plans for the future.

Happening to look up, I saw the steamer was a Mobile packet. I liked to fell off the barrel. But haste may be my own undoing, so I deliberately sat still looking quietly across the river. A hand touched my shoulder. Looking up, I stared right into the eyes of my owner, the doctor from Mobile. All he said was: "Well, well," and I climbed off the barrel completely overcome by the suddenness of my discovery.

That night I went back to Mobile with the old doctor, who was kindness itself. It was by the rarest accident he stumbled onto me, as he had given up ever seeing me again. After months of absence and adventure I found myself back in Mobile, at my starting point. However skeptical one may be of my story up to date, the facts and episodes happened quite in the way I have narrated them. If the records of Mobile are extant they will verify my existence and what followed.

SIX

MY OLD DOCTOR was true to his promise he made to me in New Orleans, that I would not be tried or punished for my beating the woman who kept the slave hospital. On the other hand he took great interest in me. I am sure he knew I was reading his books, though he never hinted at the matter. In every other way my life was as pleasant as though I had never been away. But my kind old master knew of the time to come for me, so again he advised me to learn a trade.

This time he placed me with a friend of his, the owner of an iron foundry. I was to learn the trade of an iron molder. It was [a] natural bent, so I went at it with a will, so that I was soon a full-fledged molder.[13]

Being of an inventive turn of mind, as you will see later, I soon rigged up my bench so I could do more and better work than any man in the shop. This fact naturally caused some ill feeling among the other workmen towards me.

My master gave me what I made, so I very foolishly spent my money on myself. I remember I paid $20 for a hat. My extravagance caused the foreman to complain to the superintendent, who warned me that I was playing a game that would eventually lead me into trouble. Instead of heeding his advice,

I went right on squandering my earnings, heaping up trouble for myself.

By this time I must have become not only extravagant but quite impudent. One morning I arrived at the foundry a little late. I had on my good clothes, of which I was exceedingly proud. The superintendent, who was on the crane lifting a heavy casting, called to me to come help. I called to him as soon as I put on my overalls that I would come. This apparent insubordination threw him into a rage.

By this time I was angry myself, so I told him I would come when I changed my clothes and not before. This so angered him he lashed at me and struck me in the face. I struck back and the next thing I knew, I was in a regular knock-down-and-drag-out fistfight. That was the end of me. That night my friend and master told me he was going to send me to a friend of his in New Orleans, who was also the owner of an iron foundry, until my trouble would blow over.

Monday morning I was in New Orleans, at the iron foundry. I was put to work under a foreman who did not know his job. I knew then that my position was hopeless, because I knew I was a good workman, and would put him to shame, through the kind of work the foreman was turning out. Sure enough I lasted just one week. Saturday night I was dismissed. But dismissal was nothing to what followed, since I was told that my master had sent word, if I did not get along, I was to be sold as a field hand.

When Mr. Jennings, the man's name, went out of his office, I followed close on his heels, determined to make one more appeal to my good master in Mobile. When I arrived in Mobile the next morning, my doctor friend absolutely refused to hear my side of the case. The only promise I could get out of him was that on Wednesday, I would be sent back to Mr. Jennings in New Orleans.[14] I knew that meant the cotton fields of Alabama would see my finish.

Seeing my pleadings with the doctor were futile, I decided

to take my case in my own hands. Among the people I knew in Mobile was a widow named Mrs. Ryder. She was a patient of the doctor's, so I had been to her home a number of times. To her I now went asking her to buy my freedom, letting me pay her back from my earnings.

She was frank enough to tell me that the proposition did not appeal to her, because I was always in trouble, and could not keep a job. From her I went to several other wealthy people, but received absolutely no encouragement. I was a dog with a bad name, which was in fact very bad. Tuesday night saw me in the depths of despair. I begged the doctor [to] give me a week, but he was immovable. It was Wednesday for New Orleans, and that was final.

Wednesday morning when I went to make a final plea to Mrs. Ryder, she refused to see me. I was desperate, so I held on, until she finally agreed to see me. She apparently was not interested in me, still holding to the fact that however good a workman I might be, I could not hold my job. I finally made her the proposition that while I was sure I could pay her back in two years, I would stay on another year if she would only buy my freedom.

It was my persistency that finally won her consent, rather than her cupidity, for she agreed to release me as soon as I had paid her in full. My contract all signed and agreed to called for the payment of $1,800, with interest, to be paid at the rate of $10 per week. That day I became the slave of Mrs. Ryder. My friend the doctor was pleased with the deal, as he knew I would have a good home. So we parted as good friends, which he always was to me.

Mrs. Ryder gave me a free hand to go where I wanted to and do as I pleased. She was just as good to me as the doctor, but she had no library, which was a direct loss to me. Fortunately, there was a vacancy in a Mobile foundry that was very busy, and short of molders. I was employed by piecework, so

the more castings I turned out the greater my pay. That plan
suited me fine.

Long before the other workmen were around in the morning, I was hard at work over my molds. The days were too
short. On Sundays, I met the steamers with my wheelbarrow,
ready to deliver packages or trunks. In addition to my work in
the foundry, I ran a regular three-ball pawnshop,[15] buying and
selling anything and everything offered me.

Each week I not only paid my installment [but also] frequently doubled it, so at the end of six months I had made a
very substantial payment on my contract. Mrs. Ryder was
pleased and I was more delighted at the prospect of my early
freedom. At this time I was 18,[16] strong as an ox, and working
like a steam engine, under high pressure. Another six months
would see me in sight of the end of slavery.

I had been quietly working for some time on a new idea of
a circular harrow or clod smasher, which was a very important
farm implement of that period with so much new land to
break up. Being handy with tools, on my own time I secretly
made a model. It looked so good I showed it to the superintendent, who took it so much to heart, I never saw my model
again. I went to the owner of the foundry, who in turn called
in the superintendent. In my presence the superintendent
claimed both the idea and model were his, and that I had
nothing to do with the development of the machine. The
words were hardly out of his mouth when I had him by the
throat. If I had been normal, I never would have done such a
senseless thing like that. But I had hopes that my invention
would not only pay me out of slavery, but give a start when I
was free. As it was, the treachery of the man was more than
my overwrought nerves would stand.

I hurried home and told Mrs. Ryder what I had done and
why. While she was sympathetic at the same time she was so
practical, she knew what would happen to me. She advised me

to quit the foundry trade, which I was compelled to do because I was not wanted in the two foundries in Mobile. Once on the street, my position was hopeless. Even my trading schemes failed, so I was running behind [in] my contract.

But Mrs. Ryder was a good woman. She encouraged me all she could, never saying a word to me about my lapse in payments. To add to my cup of bitterness, passing by the foundry, I saw at least seven of my clod crushers packed and ready for shipment. I stopped and counted them over and over again. The profits on that shipment would have practically wiped out my indebtedness, but I passed on a slave and a beggar.

Then I had a real break in my string of ill luck. A new foundry was starting. They needed molders and I applied for a job and got it at once. The next morning I was around as soon as the doors were opened, once more alert and hopeful. The first week I lived in that shop. Early and late I was at my bench. Every penny went to my benefactress. In exactly 18 months after I had entered into the contract with Mrs. Ryder, I made my last payment to her, starting forth a free man.

She wanted me to stay on, as I had been an exceedingly handy man about the house. But I had other plans. I wanted to get on in life, and I knew with all her best wishes Mobile was a poor place for me to stop. As soon as my free papers were signed, I asked for a passport[17] to Jeffersonville, Indiana, where I had been told there were iron foundries.

Then I did a foolish thing. Being free, I went around to gloat over the man who stole my clod smasher. Upon entering the shop the first thing that struck my eye was a row of my machines, with a lot of castings for more on the floor. The superintendent was not pleased to see me, for the wretch's conscience troubled him for his defrauding me.

However, I told him I was free, and was leaving for the north. He demanded to see my papers. I told him they were sewn in my clothes, that they had been passed upon by the authorities and they were in order. He was determined to cause me trouble. So rather than give him that satisfaction, I ruined my new clothes, by ripping out the lining.

After looking at them a few minutes, he sneeringly put them in his jacket, saying they were not worth the paper they were written on. For once I controlled my temper, knowing Mrs. Ryder would make good any irregularities that might exist in the papers already issued.

Sure enough Mrs. Ryder did make good the fault, and again I sewed the papers in my clothes. Now I determined on my revenge on the man who had caused me all the trouble. I knew he was the last man to leave the foundry at night. Biding my time, I stepped through the door into the shop in time to catch him alone. I took off my coat and vest. He was no coward and knew what was coming. I told him I was leaving Mobile forever. Before I left I was going to give him a good beating or he was going to perform [one] upon me.

It was a fight to a finish. The molds were off the floor so we had ample space to fight. I had been through too many rough-and-tumble fights not to know the tricks of combat. With the notice I had given my man, it was impossible for me to get in the first blow, which is a very [important] point in this sort of contest. It was now a fight man to man. As I have said, my man was no coward, was strong, and willing to fight. We plunged at each other again and again, our arms working like flails. I only had one thing in mind and that was his treachery, and this was my last chance at him.

I am very sure my will to beat him kept me on my feet. In one of my rushes, my opponent's impetus carried him over me, throwing him heavily to the hard floor. I was on him like a flash. When he staggered up I hit him fairly on the jaw, knocking him down again. Then I knew he was done for, but he was game and came back for more. But the animal in me knew no pity. As he arose I swung hard on his jaw. He trembled all over. Then I hit him again with every ounce of vengeance I could muster. This time he went down for good. I gloated over his bruised face, discolored eyes. As a free man, I had met him fairly and asserted my superiority . . . [over] a contemptible foe.

Hurrying home, I found Mrs. Ryder at home. I told her frankly of my fight and the necessity of my catching the New Orleans steamer that evening. She urged me to stay and meet the difficulty, but I made up my mind to go.

I bade her goodbye, with regrets because of her almost motherly kindness. I then went to see my old master the doctor, because I did owe so much to him. He knew I had been fighting again. Without knowing any of the details, he advised me to leave Mobile at once and not stop until I had reached one of the free states.

So far as my masters were concerned, most of my life as a slave was a pleasant one, so far as my bodily wants were concerned. But I hated the injustices and restraints against my own initiative more than it is possible for words to express. To me that was the great curse of slavery. If I had submitted, I presume I would have been a good house servant, but my independent nature would not permit [me] to do so humbly. I never saw either my benefactor or benefactress again.

That night I left quietly for New Orleans. The next day I was safely aboard an upriver Mississippi River packet on my way to Jeffersonville, Indiana. On the way up the river I tried to locate various points of my previous adventure, but I was unable to do so. At Jeffersonville I went to work as a molder. I found my work agreeable; but for my wandering desires, I supposed I would have stayed there all my life. But Cincinnati lured my away to other adventures.

SEVEN

AS A BACKGROUND to my adventures which follow, it is
necessary to digress at this time, otherwise you would never
be able to interpret or understand the new field into which I
entered; also what it meant to me and the people I served.
What I am bringing to your attention at this time is a strip of
land between the northern and southern states which I call the
Borderland. In my particular instance it was between Kentucky and Ohio, with the Ohio River flowing between.

This Borderland on the Ohio reached the top of the riverbank, while the Kentucky limits extended across the state
even into Tennessee, in fact there was no southern limits. It
was through this Borderland that slaves made their way going
north to Canada. For after the War of 1812 every slave knew
the north star led to freedom and Canada.[18] From 1812 the
gauntlet of war was thrown down between the friends and
enemies of the fugitive, and [there was] incessant warfare,
much like the old Scottish incursions along the lowland British border.

Every night of the year saw runaways, singly or in groups,
making their way slyly to the country north. Traps and snares

were set for them, into which they fell by the hundreds and were returned to their homes. But once they were infected with the spirit of freedom, they would try again and again, until they succeeded or were sold south. You can imagine this game of hide-and-go-seek was not without its excitements and tragedies, which called into play the nerve and courage of good men on both sides of this danger line.

The success of the fugitives was absolutely dependent upon a few conscientious men north of the line who received no compensation, in fact, made themselves poor serving the helpless fugitives who came to their doors. The fugitives in most instances had to take care of themselves south of the line, but once across the Ohio River they were in the hands of their friends. Consequently, this whole Borderland was continuously stirred with strife and hatred over the runaways who were endeavoring to break through.

Every precaution was taken to prevent the fugitive from successfully passing through this forbidden land. The woods were patrolled nightly by constables, and any man black or white had to give a good account of himself, especially if he were a stranger. Every ford was watched, while along the creeks and the river, the skiffs were not only pulled up on shore, but were padlocked to trees, and the oars removed. There were dogs in every dooryard, ready to run down the unfortunates.

Once word came from further south that runaways were on the way, the whole countryside turned out, not only to stop the fugitives, but to claim the reward for their capture. Everything was organized against the slaves' getaway.

But in spite of the odds against them, there were a surprising number who did make good their escape. This must be said for the slaves who took to the woods, they were above the average slave in intelligence and courage, otherwise they would never have started. Once they were started, no obstacle was too great for them to overcome.

A man and his wife came to the Ohio River at night. Neither could swim a stroke. Still they were so determined, he placed his wife astride a log, while he placed his hand on the other and literally kicked his way across that deep and dangerous river.[19] When at midnight the two wet and exhausted travelers came knocking on my door, I could not believe their story that they had made their journey in the manner I have stated. However, there they were. Before morning I had fed them, dried them, and taken them over the hill to a place of safety.

A man [who had] escaped to Canada came to me on his way back to get his wife. I tried to persuade him to get another wife, but he went on and shortly returned with her. But he was a rare man.

One night I made an incursion into the enemy's country. When I came back to the river my companion failed to appear with my boat. I secured a smaller one, loaded my crowd, and found I had one too many for my craft. The man left on shore was the husband of one of the women in the boat. We were being pursued and had no time to argue the point.

As I hesitated, one of the men in the boat walked ashore to make room for the husband. While this act was contrary to the eternal law of self-preservation, this ignorant slave sacrificed his freedom, without a moment's hesitation. Unfortunately, he was captured before we got across the river, a heroic victim of his own unselfishness. So I could go on and write instances of courage and sacrifice that these runaways showed and endured in their determined effort to break away from slavery.

As I have said, the Borderland south of the Ohio River was unlimited. On the Ohio side it was limited to the doorways of houses at the top of the riverbank. Speaking within my own knowledge I can truthfully say that the real warfare was waged around these few homes. Around these their neighbors were stirred to intense and bitter feelings.

The occupants of these few homes were the midnight marauders, very secretive and silent in their ways, but trustworthy and friendly to the fugitives.[20] These friendly men was hunted by the slave owners in search of his slaves.

He was watched by his neighbors, threatened by the authorities, and frequently betrayed by his friends. His work was all done under cover of the night. He had to use all manner of subterfuges to throw his watchers off his trail. In spite of law and man, these men in spite of hardships, and beset [with] difficulties, went on year after year in the work, which he believed was his burden [and] duty to perform. And he did perform it well.

Plots and counterplots were planned and sprung by both sides, which kept those interested in the game constantly on the watch as well as on the go. The real history of these men and this period will never be told, for the principal actors have passed away, leaving here and there stray episodes, which are mere incidents of the real adventure going on behind the scenes. But the strategies resorted to, the ambushes sprung, and the actual hand-to-hand conflicts between individuals and groups in this Borderland will never be told, for the simple reason that the men who knew dare not tell what they knew.

For 20 years, from 1845 to 1865, I labored in this Borderland in and around Ripley, Ohio. In that time I knew everything that went on, whether I was a participant or not. This little town today is quiet and peaceful, with no indications of the fierce passions that disturbed its people during the period I have indicated.

There was a time, however, when fierce passions swept this little town, dividing its people into bitter factions. I never

The John P. Parker House, fronting the Ohio River, in a photograph from 1910. The John P. Parker Historical Society is seeking to restore this historic home to its nineteenth-century condition. (Ohio Historical Society)

Pages 49 and 50 of Frank Gregg's
interview with John Parker.
(The Special Collections Library,
Duke University)

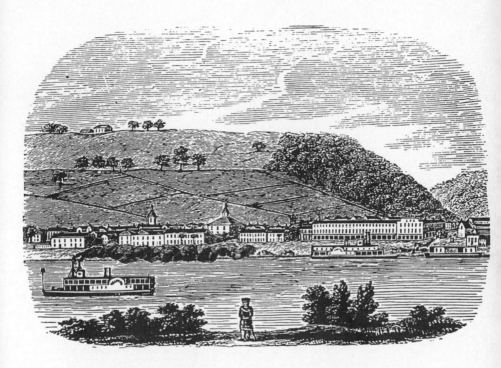

1846 engraving of Ripley, showing John Rankin's house high
on the hill. The building can still be seen for miles from across
the Ohio River, though the open fields have become woods.
(*Historical Collections of Ohio*)

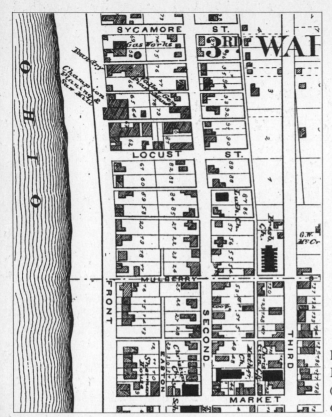

Detail from map of
Ripley, Ohio, 1876.

(D. J. Lake's *Atlas of Brown
County, Ohio*, 1876)

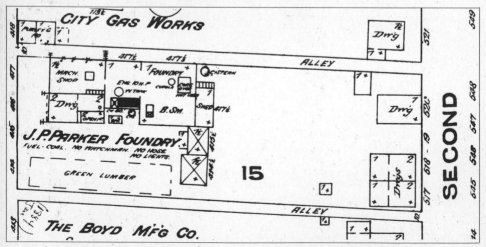

1884 map showing the layout of Parker's Phoenix Foundry.

(Sanborn Insurance Company)

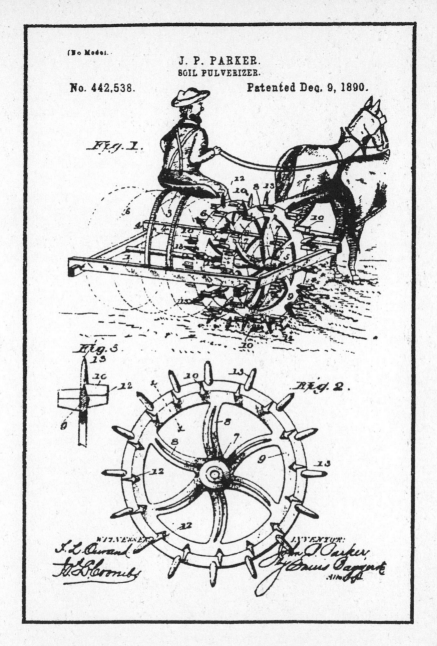

Patent for Parker's soil pulverizer. Parker's Phoenix Foundry also produced his patented tobacco press, one of which is on display at the National Underground Railroad Museum in Maysville, Kentucky. Parker was one of only fifty-five African Americans to receive patents before 1901.

Gasworks, alley, Phoenix Foundry, and Parker's house (left to right) in a photograph taken between 1865 and 1890. (Ohio Historical Society)

Thomas Collins's house, built circa 1820, photographed in 1910. Collins, a cabinet and coffin maker, was the man to whom Parker often turned when running into difficulty forwarding his fugitive slaves on from Ripley. (Ohio Historical Society)

John Rankin's grave. Rankin (1793–1886) was an active abolitionist and conductor on the Underground Railroad. (Photograph by Stuart Sprague)

Eliza's crossing. The character Eliza in Harriet Beecher Stowe's *Uncle Tom's Cabin* is believed to have been based on a woman who crossed a thawing Ohio River to this point from Kentucky, carrying her baby in her arms. She then found refuge in John Rankin's house. (Photograph by Stuart Sprague)

Hale Giddings Parker (1851–1925), John Parker's second-born
son, graduated from Oberlin College in 1873 and was the first
of the family to settle in St. Louis, Missouri. Active in politics,
he was an alternate at large to the Chicago World's Fair
Commission, and in 1894 moved to Chicago where he practiced
law. His daughters became Chicago school teachers. (St. Paul
Appeal, 1891)

Hortense Parker Gilliam (1859–1938), one of John Parker's
three daughters, graduated from Mount Holyoke College in
1883, one of the first African Americans to do so. Musically
talented, after giving piano lessons in a number of cities, she
followed her brother Hale to St. Louis. In 1913, she married
Marcus James Gilliam, Cornell Class of 1901. He spent most of
his career as a principal in the St. Louis schools. (Mount Holyoke
College Archives, circa 1930s)

Slaves who escaped to Canada. Wilbur H. Siebert, the pioneering historian of the Underground Railroad, interviewed a number of former fugitive slaves in Ontario between July 30 and August 3, 1895. It is reasonable that this photograph, which appeared in Siebert's *The Underground Railroad from Slavery to Freedom*, was taken at that time. After the 1850 Fugitive Slave Act was passed, even slaves who had escaped to Michigan and northern Ohio fled to Canada. (By permission of the Houghton Library, Harvard University (US5278 3625))

Ripley today from the Kentucky side of the Ohio River. Despite the raising of the river by a system of dams, the integrity of nineteenth-century Ripley remains intact and is being preserved by the creation of the Ripley Historic District. (Photograph by Stuart Sprague)

thought of going uptown without a pistol in my pocket, a knife in my belt, and a blackjack handy. Day or night I dare not walk on the sidewalks for fear someone might leap out of a narrow alley at me.

What I did the other men did, walked the streets armed. This was a period when men went armed with pistol and knife and used them on the least provocation. When under cover of night the uncertain steps of slaves were heard quietly seeking their friends. When the mornings brought strange rumors of secret encounters the night before, but daylight showed no evidence of the fray; when pursuers and pursued stood at bay in a narrow alley with pistols drawn ready for the assault; when angry men surrounded one of the houses referred to, kept up gunfire until late in the afternoon, endeavoring to break into it by force, in search of runaways. These were the days of passion and battle which turned father against son, and neighbor against neighbor. Visit it now to see the contrast of this picture of violence.

In this town of Ripley, there are still a few of the old houses standing, which were places of refuge for the runaway. Facing the river on the corner of First Street and Mulberry stands the old Collins house, a two-storied brick house around which are gathered many of the dramatic episodes of this period. At the top of the riverbank, its two doors, facing two different streets, made it easy access to the fleeing fugitives. The doors unlocked, lighted candle on the table, many times I have slipped into this room, surrounded by a motley group of scared fugitives. Arousing the man of the house, he would quickly feed the crowd, then take them out the back way through the alley, over the hills to Red Oak or Russellville. If this old house could only bring back its shadows, they would be many and mingled.

Further down on Front Street is the McCague house with its narrow high stoop, up whose steps many strange men and women went gently tapping on the door.[21] The cellar and the garret have been filled with breathless fugitives. Like the Collins house and all the other houses of these early abolitionists, the door was always ajar, and the candle in the room lighted and waiting to welcome any and all who entered.

But the real fortress and home to the fugitives was the house of Rev. John Rankin, perched on [a] high hill behind the town. A single-story brick house,[22] it sheltered Rev. John Rankin, a man of deeds as well as of words. If the shadows on the wall could but return, you could count the sire, with six sons, seven resolute men, holding their border castle against all comers.

At times times attacked on all sides by masters seeking their slaves, they beat back their assailant, and held its threshold unsullied.[23] A lighted candle stood as beacon which could be seen from across the river, and like the north star was the guide to the fleeing slave. In this eagle's nest, Rev. John Rankin and his sons held forth during many stormy years, and only left the old home when their work was well and lastingly done.

I am now living under my own roof, which still stands just as it did in the old strange days. I saw it grow brick by brick. It too has heard the gentle tapping of fugitives. It also has heard the cursing at the door of the angry masters. It too has played its part in concealing men and women seeking a haven of safety. Standing, facing the river, it has weathered the storms of years, very much better than its owner and builder. But we have seen adventurous nights together, which, I am glad to say, will never come again.

Ripley likewise has lost its wealth and prestige. At one time it was a rival of Cincinnati in wealth, boat building, pork packing, flatboat and steamboat landings. It was richer still in its ideals, for in 1805, years before any one [else] in the west, it gave heed to the antislavery movement, [and] Dr. Alexander Campbell, the first abolitionist of Ohio, moved into town.

Dr. Campbell was a senator from Ohio when the British burned Washington in the War of 1812. He was the first citizen of the town as well as the forerunner of the abolition movement. Around this we now rallied the group of Scotch Presbyterians who were my associates in aiding the fugitives. Indiana [and] Illinois abolitionists got their creed and leadership from the abolitionists of Ripley.

It is generally and rightfully believed that the Underground Railroad had its origin in Ripley. An old citizen who claimed to be present at the time of the incident gives the fact of its origin from personal knowledge. It was in the upper shipyard on Red Oak Creek that the episode occurred shortly after the close of the War of 1812. The fugitive ran amongst the piles of lumber and disappeared. One of the workmen, when asked by the master if he had seen the fugitive, answered, "The slave disappeared so quickly he must have gone on an underground road." The term "rail" was fixed after the introduction of steam [rail]roads.[24]

From my own personal knowledge of the men in Cincinnati and the men of Ripley, I can say that Ripley was the real terminus of the Underground Railroad. I worked with both groups [Cincinnati and Ripley] after 1845 so I ought to know. Levi Coffin, a Quaker abolitionist of Cincinnati, was the best-known antislavery leader to the nation because he had greater publicity than the men of Ripley. But he had no such group as operated in and around the latter town. That the town deserved its reputation is shown by the fact [that] it was generally known throughout Kentucky as "the hell hole of abolition."

One thing I do know [is] that it wielded more influence in the west than any other town, big or little. The work was begun by Dr. Alexander Campbell in 1805, who was practically driven out of Kentucky for his liberalism. Rev. James Gilliland came here in 1806 from North Carolina, being driven out of the presbytery, on account of his antislavery attitude.[25]

Reverend John Rankin was driven out of Kentucky, and with him came his entire congregation of farmers from near Carlisle, who settled around Greensburg, Indiana. Not only is that true, but the first textbook, "Letters to a Slave Owner," was written and published in Ripley by Reverend John Rankin. It had a wide circulation at the time and really was the foundation of the New England movement under William Lloyd Garrison. Reverend Jesse Lockhart of Russellville[26] and Dr. Lester of Decatur were associates and advocates of the Ripley group.

Do not think that Cincinnati and Ripley were the only centers of runaway activities. As a matter of fact, from the Atlantic Ocean to the Mississippi River south of the Ohio, there was a constant trickle of runaways. But for fixed permanent organization these two groups were the best-organized and the best-known.

There was a reason why Ripley was the seat of the abolition movement. This reason being it was in the center of the Virginia Military District of Ohio, which [was] set aside for the soldiers of the line of Virginia, who served in the War of the Revolution. These wild lands were the only place where the Virginia or southern masters could take their slaves and free them, without any liability to themselves.[27]

There were two settlements of free men in Brown county, of which Ripley was the river town. Here slaves were brought and freed. True, the settlements did not work out so well, but it did offer an outlet for those planters who had fought for the Declaration of Independence, and practiced its tenets.

As a matter of fact, the Ripley abolition group were the

intermediaries between the spirit of the Revolutionary patriots and the fiery New England group who took this fire and inspiration about 1830 from the irrepressible firebrand William Lloyd Garrison.

Having given you a background in Ripley, I will return to my personal experiences and adventures, in my own little personal war on slavery.

EIGHT

MY FIRST EXPERIENCE with the runaways was in 1845 in Cincinnati, where I was working at my trade as an iron molder. I was in contact with the free colored men, so I knew of Levi Coffin, the Quaker who was active and resourceful. There are said to have been 22 fugitives hid away in his house at one time.

One or two incidents might be of interest here, to show you how resourceful Levi Coffin was in his meeting difficult situations. It was at the time when he had so many fugitives he could not handle them in an ordinary way. A livery man was aroused out of his bed one night by a stranger, who wanted to hire a hearse and carriages. It was arranged that the mourners were to be picked up at a certain place outside of the city. All night long and part of the next day the carriages with drawn curtains followed the hearse until they reached Middletown, where the mourners all disappeared. Only rumor connected Levi Coffin with the affair, as the stranger paid the livery man and there was no evidence as to whom he was.[28]

The use of double-bottomed wagons was a common method for getting fugitives out of the city. Covered with hay or garden truck, the old-time huckster wagons with their curtains drawn down carried loads other than tin pans and kettles. I narrate these methods in use in thickly settled communities, to indicate how the runaways silently and secretly found their way to Toledo, Sandusky, Cleveland, or Ashtabula, which were the four ports where known steamers would take them across Lake Erie to Canada.

My first real experience with the runaways was in a manner unsought by me, in fact, I was unwillingly forced into it. I had met a freeman who was a barber, in the house where I was living. He told me that he had lived in Maysville, Kentucky, and was under suspicion of having helped runaways. He was given one night to be gone, so he took the first packet to Cincinnati, leaving his wife to pack up their belongings.

The man confided in me that several nights before he was forced to get out of town, [he] met two girls in the act of running away. Knowing that they had a good home and a kindly mistress, besides being young, he persuaded the girls to go back home and stay there. Now that he had been treated so brutally, he had made up his mind to run the girls away and proposed I accompany him back to Maysville to aid in the enterprise.

Being happy and contented, I refused to have anything to do with his proposition. The matter was dropped so far as I knew, when the barber told me one evening that he had gotten word to the girls, that he was going after them, again asking me to accompany him, and again I refused. But he kept after me so persistently, I promised to go with him.

His plan was to go to a Ohio upriver town called Ripley, of which I had never even heard. This town, he said, was ten miles below Maysville. We would make our headquarters there instead of Maysville, where he was known. His plan was to follow up the river after night [and] steal a skiff, while I went into Maysville to get the girls. On the face of it, it was quite a foolish thing for me to even try to do. But he assured me he would land me below another freeman's house, so all I had to do was to climb the bank [and] make known my mission, and the freeman would take the word to the girls.

We landed easy enough [and] he gave such [an] accurate description of the freeman's house, I felt I could find it. So we started out quite sure of our game, little thinking where our simple little affair would lead us. I found Ripley an active town, with a settlement of freemen on the side hill across the creek.

There we picked up a colored man who knew the country, who agreed to go along with us until we found our skiff, that was as far as he could go. The three of us walked up as far as Logan's Gap, which was on the Ohio side about five miles below Maysville. There we went to the riverbank to find our skiff. We searched the shore until we came to the lights of Maysville, without finding a boat. There were plenty of boats but they were padlocked so securely and their oars gone [so] we were not able to use [them]. So back into the settlement we went, where we hid during the day.

All the next night we searched fruitlessly for a boat. We did find one, which apparently had been drawn up carelessly on the shore. When we got it into the water it leaked like a sieve. Again, we turned back to Ripley to hide away. My barber friend, being discouraged, told me that unless we could find a boat this the third night he was going back to Cincinnati. We examined the shore carefully but not a boat was to be had. It would have been an easy matter to break a padlock, but lacking oars we were no better off than we were before.

On our way back we found a desirable boat with no oars. I agreed to search the yard of a house on the top of the bank. But a loud barking dog put an end to my hopes in that house. It had been raining most of the night, so when we got back to Ripley, my barber friend was not only exhausted, but firmly set in his mind he was through. Having set my face towards a goal, I was determined to make another try at it, [even] if I had to go alone. In spite of my pleading and ridiculing him, my associate did take the boat back to Cincinnati; leaving me alone.

Fortunately, in our excursions up the river he located the house of the freeman, which was in a settlement of his own color. So I had no fear but I could handle that end of the affair by myself. I decided to boldly go direct to Maysville, thence to the freemen's settlement, working directly from there. I had little trouble in finding my man, but he absolutely refused to have anything to do with the enterprise, and advised me to leave.

It was only after I had given his friend's name, and the names of the two girls, and my story of how I had been inveigled into the enterprise, that he would even listen to me. Then all he would agree to do was to show me where I could get a boat, where the oars were hid; I could do the rest myself. He did agree to have the girls down to the boat at a certain hour that night. With that I had to be content.

At the appointed hour I was in the boat waiting. Shortly afterwards, two figures came stealthily down the bank. One was short, the other tall, but both were unusually fat. When the girls came to me I understood what gave them their unusual size.

They had on not only their mistress' tilter hoops, one had on four dresses, the other confessed to three and much underwear. What to do with these two stuffed figures was a problem. For when I tried to put both of them in the stern where they belonged, they filled the boat to running over with hoop skirts.

I finally arranged the matter by placing one in each end of the boat. In addition to this extra clothing each had brought a bundle almost as large as herself filled with trinkets and satin slippers, and other truck down to a frying pan, with which they proposed to fry their bacon on the road.

Any other time I would have laughed, but serious work, and dangerous work to me, was at hand. I refused to carry the plunder and was about to throw it into the river when the two got up such a cry, I had to push off and leave it on the bank. Even then they were brokenhearted over leaving their loot behind and were even surly to me over their loss. There was no time to lose as I had to row ten miles, and get the girls out of sight before daylight.

I rowed to the Ohio side, where I was more or less familiar owing to my three nightly excursions along that shore. Just before I reached Logan's Gap, a low pass through the high hills, I heard the rhythmical beat of oars back of us. Then I knew the bundles left behind had told their deadly story.

My only safety was ashore. I made the girls take off their extra clothing and throw them in the bottom of the boat. The girl in the bow became entangled in her hoop skirts and fell overboard with a yell that echoed in the hills. When I stopped to fish the girl out of the river, I lost one of my oars, so I had to paddle ashore.

We had shipped so much water in the rescue, the girls were compelled to use their mistress' fine bonnets to bail out the water. As we reached the shore the girl in the bow leaped out, upsetting the boat, throwing me into the river. I let the skiff float off as I scrambled ashore.

By this time we could hear the frantic efforts of our pursuers distinctly, though I could not see them. At this point, while the bank was low, it was very steep. The tall girl clambered up the bank without much trouble, but the short one could not make it. She started to scream, but I slapped my hand over her mouth and threatened to strangle her, shutting her up in a hurry. Between the tall girl pulling and my pushing we got the girl up the bank, hoop skirts and all.

There was a cornfield across the bottoms, reaching to the foot of the hills. Through that cornfield, the tall girl with her hoop skirts drawn up about as high as her head went like a scared rabbit. But the short girl was in trouble again. Losing sight of us, she began to scream again. This time I shut her up by telling her if she opened her mouth again I would leave her to shift for herself. I then made her take off all her dresses except one. Reduced of her load, she was able to keep up with me.

When we reached the hill we heard our pursuers yelling, so I felt they had discovered our boat, which fortunately for us, the current had carried downstream. I had carried the dresses I had made the short girl take off. At the same time I knew there was a swath through the cornfield as big as a bull elephant could make.

Clinging to a well-traveled road, I made the girls follow along this until daylight began to break. I knew we could not make Ripley, so I turned back, carefully concealing our trail where we left the road. I climbed halfway up the hill and hid in a clump of bushes.

Overcome by the excitement of the chase, I fell asleep. In the middle of the afternoon, a man whom I afterwards knew as Ben Sidwell was calling his hogs. I was so sure we would be discovered, I drew a large knife, determined to kill him. Fortunately for both of us, he went up the hill hallooing for his hogs.

Shortly after dark we arrived at the colored settlement on the side of the hill overlooking Ripley. The man I wanted was awake. He told me there was a terrible row in town over our escape, that the Theodore Collins place, which was just over the top of the hill, was being watched, that officers had searched the colored settlement and were on watch for us.

He would not leave his house in our company but told me to take the girls and hide under the Third Street bridge across

Red Oak Creek and wait until later, when he would take a chance of guiding us to a friend. It must have been midnight when he came whistling down the road. Stopping on the bridge, after making sure he was not being followed, [he] called to me.

Then it was that he pointed out a light on top of the hill, where he said we would find friends. He whistled aloud while we followed through the streets of the town. For some reason of his own, our guide took us right through the town, down Third Street to Mulberry, down Mulberry to the Collins house. He walked in without knocking. We were right on his heels. To my surprise there was a light lit. Tapping on a bed-room door, Eli Collins came out.

Taking us into the kitchen, he had the girls prepare a good meal. The last I ever saw or heard of the two girls was when they were following Eli Collins down a back alleyway. He told me afterwards that he took them to the house of Reverend James Gilliland at Red Oak Chapel. That was my forcible introduction to Ripley and the Underground Railroad.

NINE

THE FIRST ADVENTURE prompted me to move to Ripley, where there was an iron foundry. To give you the real background of my activities, it is necessary to tell you about Ripley in 1845. At that time it was as busy as a beehive. There was no town along the Ohio River except Cincinnati that was in its class. There was a group of live men there that made it the center of industry and finance. There was Samuel Hemphill,[29] Archibald Leggett,[30] the Boyntons, Thomas McCague,[31] James Reynolds were the leaders.

There were the upper and lower boatyards, busy the year round. The upper boatyard was the oldest and larger of the two, located at the mouth of Red Oak Creek. There was a jut of land below the creek which gave the boatyard a safe harbor, winter and summer.[32] One hundred flatboats were made here in one year for Vevay, Indiana, to float hay down the river. These boats were turned out in quantities and very rapidly all winter long. The mills would turn out the parts, so all that would have to be done in the spring and summer was to assemble the parts into flatboats.

These boats were assembled bottom side up. When they

slid down the way, they were upset so they floated right side up. In winter steamboats were on the ways. The entire riverfront was filled with flatboats loading cargoes for New Orleans and all waypoints. Winter and summer there flowed down the river highways into the town a continuous stream of logs night and day. Only pork was packed, as the south did not feed beef to its slaves. The slaughterhouses were in full blast at all seasons. Flour mills, both water and steam, ground up the grain of the neighboring farms, which were very fertile. One mill located back from the river had an overhead gravity runway, sending the barrels from the mill across the creek down to the bank to the flatboats.

All winter long the farmer and his family were busily engaged making pork and flour barrels, and tobacco hogsheads. These were brought to town either on sleighs or by four-to-six-horse teams. At times the farmers killed [and] packed their own hogs. A woolen mill made most of the jeans for the town and flatboats.

There were still Jacksonian gentlemen who wore blue jean suits with brass buttons and swallow coattails, who devoted as much time to keeping their long rows of brass buttons shining as the men of today to preening and cleaning.[33]

This little town was so rich [that] in the Panic of 1837, it sent its funds to help New York banks over that depression.[34] It was as busy as a beehive and as thrifty as it was busy.[35]

I must make a passing observation that it is now 60 years after the time I have just been dealing with.[36] All the boatyards are gone. The flatboats have disappeared years ago, not even a steamboat can be seen. That group of able financiers and businessmen are gone and with one exception not a kith or kin of those busy men is left in town.

The men and women of the metropolis of Ripley have passed on. Hardly a memory of them now exists, except in the mind of a few aged citizens like myself. So quickly does our country change in its centers of trade but [also] in its methods of trade. But the Ohio River still remains a thing of real beauty to me.

Amidst this commercial activity lived and moved the little group of old-time abolitionists. They were by name Dr. Alexander Campbell, Rev. John Rankin, Theodore, Tom, and Eli Collins, Tom McCague, Dr. Beasley, [and] Rev. James Gilliland. The undoubted leader was Rev. John Rankin.

While the businessmen were not abolitionists, they were antislavery. But the town itself was proslavery as well as the country around it. In fact, the country was so antagonistic to abolitionism at this time, we could only take the fugitives out of town and through the country along definite and limited routes.

There was also very active a certain group of men who made a living by capturing the runaway slaves and returning them to their masters. These men were on watch day and night along the riverbank the year round. While they captured quite a few it was remarkable how many slaves we got through the line successfully. The feeling grew so tense Rev. John Rankin and his followers left the Presbyterian church forming a new congregation who were given over to the antislavery movement.

Many of the Methodists were in silent sympathy with the movement, [and] would give us money, but would take no aggressive part. As a matter of fact, this abolitionist group were ridiculed, detested, and even threatened by the town's people.

After the passage of the Fugitive Slave Law in [1850], the attitude of the town's people grew even more critical of our group.[37] We had to be more secretive than ever, for it meant confiscation of property, a fine, and [a] jail sentence.

I had kept a diary giving the names, dates, and circumstances of all the slaves I had helped run away, which at that

time numbered 315. As I had accumulated considerable property, as a matter of safety I threw this diary into the iron
furnace, for fear it might fall into other hands.

The other men were equally as cautious, but the work went
on just the same. Having now become actively engaged in
aiding the fugitives, my contact with the other abolitionists
was close, and maintained until the close of the Civil War.

Now to an adventure that required all my skill and
resourcefulness to get out of a bad situation. Tom Collins,
the coffin maker, came to me [one] night very much excited,
bringing with him one of the freemen of the town. His agitation was due to a message which this freeman had given him,
to the effect that there was a party of refugees hiding in the
woods in Kentucky about 20 miles from the river.

The word was that the slaves were from the central Kentucky [area, and] had made their way to where they were,
when their leader was captured. With no one to guide them
they were helpless. It was one of those "grape vine" dispatches,
given by word of mouth from one friend to another until it
mysteriously got across the river.

Being new and zealous in this work, I volunteered to go to
the rescue. As my mission was a dangerous one, I put a pair
of pistols in my pockets and a knife in my belt, ready for
emergencies. The colored man himself was a slave and lived
across the river in Kentucky. He had stolen a boat to bring the
message to us, so that I accompanied him in it across the river.

He furthermore assured me he would take me to the cabin
of another colored slave, who would guide me to the fugitives.
It was about daylight by the time we reached my guide, who
hid me away in the woods. That night we found the party in
the midst of the deep woods, scared and perfectly helpless.
There were ten in all, which included two women and their
husbands.

They were paralyzed with fear since the loss of their leader, and huddled together like children. They were so badly demoralized some of them wanted to give themselves up, rather than face the unknown. Food had been supplied by friends, so they were well fed, otherwise I could not have done a thing with them.

One of the men set up a wail when I had them ready to start. Drawing a pistol I sternly gave him the choice of picking up his things and coming along, or be shot down in cold blood. After that show of force, I had my charges under my control. It was a fortunate thing for me I did, as you will soon see.

My guide could not stay with me, as he had to be back home by daylight. We dared not follow the road with our party, because we were in the Borderland, which was thoroughly patrolled, and we were likely to run on one of the guards at any turn of the road. Going through the brush was hard and exhaustive labor. With the exception of a clearing now and then, dense woods extended about to the river, so we could with care travel in the daytime. It was dangerous but I soon saw it was a chance I had to take.

They were hopeless woodsmen; try as I would, I could not keep them from breaking down the bushes [and] stepping on dry sticks, the cracking of which echoed through the woods like an alarm bell. I soon discovered I would have to keep them in the ravines where the ferns and moss grew. Instead of being demoralized, they now became buoyant and . . . [hopeful] over their prospects.

In spite of my warnings, one of the single men, being thirsty, decided he would look for a spring. Again I begged him to stay by the party. As he insisted I had to let him go. Fortunately, I moved the party ahead. He had hardly got out of sight when I heard him shout. And [he] came racing through the brush pursued by two white men.

As soon as I heard the shout I made my party lie down. The

man, forgetting the location of our party, went flying by where we were lying. Shortly there was a shot, which I could see disturbed my crowd. Drawing my pistol I quietly told them I would shoot the first one that dared make a noise, which had a quieting effect.

Shortly, there was a cracking of the brush. Peering cautiously through the bushes, I saw our man being led by a rope. He had his arms tied behind his back. Evidently, the fugitive had not betrayed the presence of his friends, because the three men went on their way, looking neither to the right or left, and were soon lost in the undergrowth. It was a mighty narrow escape for me and my party, for had we gone straight ahead, we would have all been trapped and captured.

Not knowing how soon the captured man might tell of the presence of the party, I decided to get as far away from this spot as I could. Ordering the crowd to their feet, I impressed upon them that I was in greater danger than they were, and that unless they listened to me, I would leave them just where they were and save myself.

Everything went well until we came to a road. Hiding my party, I advanced to make a survey of the situation. I found a well-traveled road which I was sure I could not get across in daylight. Now the party wanted to push ahead, and it was only after more threats that I got [them] safely into the brush. It was a good thing that we did, for we had hardly hid before a party of white men on horseback passed along in sight of where I was lying. From time to time wagons rumbled by, so that I did not dare to let any of my party get out of sight, in fact move without my consent.

We made the river all right, but I was 24 hours ahead of my schedule, as Tom Collins had not figured I would travel by daylight. Consequently, there was no boat awaiting our arrival. I had no other alternative than to push straight down the bank and take my chances. My chances proved very poor, because I ran into a patrol. Seeing the size of our party he turned and ran away. I knew that the whole countryside would soon be buzzing like a hornet's nest.

Making my people throw away their bundles, I started along the bank as fast as I could go, with the fugitives following. I could see the lights of the town, but they might as well have been [on] the moon so far as being a relief to me, in my present situation. I knew there were always boats about the ferry landing. My one hope was to beat my pursuers to them. One of the women fell exhausted.

I only stopped long enough to tell her to follow us if she could, because I could not wait. Sure enough, at the ferry I found one lone boat. The next thing was to find the oars. I sent the whole crowd stomping through the brush in search of them.

While we were wildly searching, I heard the cry of hounds. The patrol had worked faster than I thought. Leaping into the boat to tear up a seat to use as a paddle, I stumbled over the oars, which I had missed finding in the dark. With a halloo, I piled the crowd into the boat, only to find it so small it would not carry all of us. Two men were left on the bank.

As I started to push off, leaving the poor fellows on the bank to their cruel fate, one of the women set up a cry that one of the men on the bank was her husband. Then I witnessed an example of heroism and self-sacrifice that made me proud of my race. For one of the single men safely in the boat, hearing the cry of the woman for her husband, arose without a word [and] walked quietly to the bank. The husband sprang into the boat as I pushed off.[38]

As I rowed away to safety I saw dimly the silent but helpless martyr. We were still far from the Ohio shore when I saw lights around the spot where we had left the man, followed by shouts, [by] which I knew the poor fellow had been captured in sight of the promised land.

Collins was surprised as well as glad to see me. We decided, in view of the alarm, both of us had better send the party to the home of Rev. James Gilliland at Red Oak Chapel, about five miles from town. There we left them, which was the last time we ever saw or heard of that crowd.

TEN

IT IS HARDLY necessary for me to say, that I am making no effort to give in detail [accounts of] the many men and women whom I helped escape into Canada in this journal. It was only now and then anything unusual came to me. In the main my work was to continuously get the fugitives out of town, see them safely [passed on to agents of the Underground Railroad].*

* *

The fiery cross of Scotland never traveled faster than the reports of these events. They were discussed in the streets of the city, the cabins of woodsmen, and they penetrated the remote corners of the Union. The south land became excited and swore vengeance on abductors and their abettors, and after every event there was an explosion of ill feeling, which found vent in angry threats.

I cite these incidents to show what danger one encountered who deliberately sought and ran away fugitives. In spite of

*From this point until page 116, we are missing pages from Gregg's interview with Parker. We have taken the appropriate pages from Gregg's work "The Borderlands," which is based on his interview with Parker.

threats and dangers a number of men in the Borderland were constantly rounding up parties and frequently going after them to lead them secretly across the Ohio. There was an excitement about the game that appealed to me, in my younger days, and I really believe I enjoyed the nightly adventures with my ever-changing flock.

By this time I had become proprietor of an iron foundry. I had married and purchased a home next to my place of business, both of which were located on the bank of the river. There was working for me a man who lived across the river in Kentucky [and] whose father owned several people.[39]

This man kept chiding me about my habits of prowling around at night, taking charge of fugitives. I stoutly denied such proclivities, but from time to time he would come back to the subject, until one day he said to me, "You are such a brave fellow, why don't you run away some of the old man's people?" I promptly disclaimed any such purpose, but at the same time I secretly vowed I would take him at his word.

Shortly after dark the same day, I loosened my skiff and made my way slowly across the river, landing below a road that led up to the house of my friend. The purpose of my excursion was to get in touch, if possible, with some of the people whom I hoped to run off.

Pulling my skiff on shore, I quietly stole up to the top of the bank and came into the road. The trees grew on both sides of the highway, making it quite dark. Being on hostile soil, I was careful to keep in the grass rather than on the hard road, where my footsteps could be heard. It was fortunate I took this precaution, for I had hardly gone a quarter of a mile when I heard voices ahead of me. Secreting myself in the bushes, I waited to see who the men were.

Shortly afterwards my friend came in sight, puffing away at a cigar. He was accompanied by one of his father's men, in fact, the very one I wished to see. The two went down the road to the river. As I was in a safe hiding place, I decided to stay and await results.

In a very short time one of the men came back. It was so dark I could not see who it was, but as the man was not smoking, I felt sure it was the one I wanted. Being somewhat in doubt, I left him go by. As soon as he had passed I slipped out and followed him until we came to a clearing, when I distinctly saw I was on the heels of a white man.

Darting to one side of the road into the bushes, I made such a racket he stopped and began whistling for his dogs, which he thought were following him and had made the noise. I waited until he went on, and then hurried back to my skiff, breathing easier after my close call.

My narrow escape made me more cautious than ever the next night, when I went back to communicate with my man. The quarters were so close to the house that I did not dare go to the cabins, but contented myself with lying in the bushes along the road, waiting an opportunity to speak to the man.

It was the third night before my chance came, then, like the first time I saw them, the two men came down the road and passed me. I hurried to a cornfield near the highway, where, hiding in the fence corner, I could get a good view of anyone passing by before I spoke.

In a little while I saw a figure coming back. I lay with both eyes peering through the cracks of the rail fence, anxiously waiting for a good look at the man's face. This time I saw plainly it was the one I wanted. As he came opposite me, without moving, I called to him softly. At that period of time men were not startled by being called by name at any time or place. So when I spoke the second time, the man stopped, and after looking around, said for me to go into the woods and he would meet me.

He walked on for a short distance, then turned and came back. In the meantime I hurried as fast as I could to the woods, keeping within the shadow of the fence.

Once within the protection of the forest I came out on the highway, and waited for my man to return. He came back leisurely so as not to excite suspicion. You may imagine he was curious to know who I was and what was wanted. He knew me by reputation, so when I gave him my name he desired no further credentials.

When I told him I wanted to run him away, he said he had a wife and a little baby, and would not go and leave them. Being determined to execute my plan, I asked him to be ready to go the following night. I would take them all. He fell in with my scheme, and before we parted it was all arranged. He was to meet me at the same place a week later, claiming he could not be ready in a day.

These plans had hardly been arranged when my companion startled me by giving a shriek and starting down the road as fast as his legs would carry him.

Glancing hastily around to see what had caused his alarm, I was just in time to see a man with a club raised ready to strike me. My opponent was so close I barely had time to dodge the blow which was aimed at my head, receiving it upon the left shoulder. The weight of the stick staggered me.

My assailant, thinking he had me under his control, attempted to trip me to the ground at the same time. I was in a desperate plight and I knew it; it was not [the] time for gentle blows and explanations.

When my assailant dropped the stick I felt it was a fair fight. What advantage he had in his hold on me was only momentary, for being of muscular build, I broke away from him with ease.

When he saw I was not going to be an easy victim, he made for his club, and as he stooped over to pick it up, I leaped on his back, forcing his face into the dirt of the road. Grabbing a handful of dust, I turned the man over and threw it in his face

and eyes. Having blinded my assailant for a moment, I broke
away and ran down the road to my boat.

It all happened so quickly I did not have a chance to see
who my assailant was. When out on an expedition, it was my
usual custom to wear different clothes and a different hat than
usual, so that my failure to recognize the man I thought was
good evidence that he did not identify me.

I felt rather queer when I went into the shop the next morning and confronted my workman from Kentucky. He was
plainly not my assailant, as his face showed no evidence of the
encounter of the night before. He was not suspicious of me in
the least, for he greeted me as usual, much to my surprise.
Later in the day, one of my men came to see me with the story
of how a patrol got into a fight with a fugitive the night
before, across the river, and lost his man. My relief can be
better imagined than expressed.

Strange as it may seem, on the morning of the day I was to
meet the man and his family, the Kentuckian chided me about
not being able to run away any of his people. I told him I was
too busy with the foundry to give attention to outside affairs.
He chuckled to himself over the matter as if it was a good joke
on me.

Owing to the sudden termination of my conference with the
would-be fugitive on the night I was attacked by the patrol, I
was not sure that my man would keep his appointment. Since
I had run such risks in the case, I was determined now to carry
the project through at any cost.

True to my word, a week later I was at the appointed place
to meet my party of runaways. This time I concealed my boat
carefully, for I wanted no miscarrying of my plans, and after
lying in the bushes for a while, my man not showing up, I
decided to go after him. It was ticklish work, but I felt it to
be necessary if I expected to carry out my plan.

There was quite an open space between the woods and the

cabins. Instead of following the road, I went in the shadows of the trees coming out to the field back of the quarters. As the corn was half grown, I had no difficulty working up to the row of log cabins.

There was a glow of candles through the windows of the big house, which surprised me at such an hour of the night. I came up opposite the cabins and stood looking at them, wondering how I was going to be able to find which one my man lived in. While I was hesitating, the door of one of the shacks opened, and my man came out. He walked up and down in front of his cabin nervously several times, then started for the cornfield.

As the man was by himself I felt sure there was something wrong, since the understanding between us was that he was to bring his wife and child to the rendezvous. Halfway between his cabin and the field, he stopped and listened for a moment, and then hurried to conceal himself in the growing corn. He entered in touching distance of where I was standing, so I had no trouble in stopping him.

Things had gone wrong, just as I supposed. The man was so scared he could hardly talk to me. He said since the night of the interview, he had been under watch. The folks in the big house had a suspicion he and his wife were planning to run away, and as a precaution compelled him to bring the baby to them every night. The little one was placed at the foot of the bed in which the owner and his wife slept. The old man had placed a chair at his side, on which was a lighted candle and a pistol, and threatened to shoot the first person he found in the room after dark. Besides, a close watch had been kept on all of the cabins to see that none of their occupants were abroad at night. While he was talking he was looking around constantly, as if he expected someone to swoop down on us.

After hearing his story I told him to go back to his home [and] blow the lights out, leaving his door open so I could enter without attracting attention. Asking no questions as to my purpose, he returned and soon had his cabin in darkness. Getting as near his house as I could under cover of the corn, I hurried across the open space and pushed my way into the room, where the man and his wife were awaiting me.

Without wasting time, I proposed that the two of them go with me, leaving the baby behind. This the woman would not listen to; her mother love prompted her to select bondage with her little one rather than freedom without it. When I endeavored to open the subject again she became hysterical for fear I was going to compel her to go against her will. Seeing my efforts were unavailing, I dropped the discussion.

I then proposed to the man that he enter the sleeping room of the big house and rescue the baby from the foot of the bed. This he refused to do, as he was afraid of the big pistol at his owner's head. I attempted to bolster up his courage by holding up to him the hopes of freedom, but he was not to be moved.

As I did not feel it was my duty to endanger my life as well as my liberty on their behalf, I pressed the woman to go to the rescue of the baby. I think she would have made the effort, but for her husband, who was thoroughly cowed by the fear of the man of the house.

When I urged her again she hesitated, and as she faltered the man broke in, saying that they were not anxious to leave and thought they better not try. From the tenor of the talk I knew that nothing could be expected from them, and any effort of rescue must come from myself. To press them further meant that they would abandon the trip, and I would return home empty-handed.

Having gone this far I decided to go all the way, enter the forbidden room, and rescue the child from the bed. Coming to this decision, I made them get their possessions in readiness to move. The woman, who was a servant in the house, described its interior, which was very simple indeed. From the small porch at the rear of the house, she said a door opened into a large living room. From this a door led into the sleeping apartment where the child was to be found. There were no locks on any of the doors, [they] being held by wooden latches.

With these facts known, I began to make my plans. I informed both of them I was going to take the child if I could. In the meantime they were to take their position in the road below the house. If they heard any shooting, they were to go back to their cabin at once and I would take care of myself. At all events they were not to take chances of discovery, for fear it might spoil future plans. With these final instructions, I took off my shoes, handing them to the man, impressing him with the fact that in case of trouble, he was to take them back to his hut and destroy them.

Together we left the cabin. The man and the woman went through the field to take their station on the road. I started for the house, going directly to it from the quarters. As I approached the place I could see the candle glow through one window and I knew that was the sleeping room. Getting into the shadow of the house, I endeavored to peep in, but the curtains were pulled down, shutting off my view. There was nothing for me to do but make my way into the place and trust to my good fortune to pull me through.

Crossing the porch, I came to the kitchen door, which I found unlocked as the woman told me. Raising the latch, I pushed it open and entered the room. I was careful to leave the door wide open so that my retreat in that direction was assured. Standing on the threshold of this strange house, I am frank to say I felt the graveness of my position. For a moment my nerve left me, and I am positive I would have run at the least noise.

As my eyes became used to the darkness of the place, my courage came back to me. The floor of the kitchen was of rough boards, so that my footing was uncertain. As I picked my way across the room it seemed to me I struck every loose board in the place. The large crack at the bottom of the door of the sleeping room, through which the rays of the candle showed, guided me surely to my destination.

At the door I hesitated, for I felt I was taking my life in my hand in opening it. If I only knew whether the man was a sound or a light sleeper, it would have eased my mind just then. The wife too was an unknown quantity. These and a multitude [of] other things came to my mind as I stood with my hand on the latch of the sleeping room, ready to open it, to an unknown fate. Twice I put pressure on the latch and twice my heart failed me. The third time my thumb pushed down on the fastening, and it gave way. It was the last point at which I hesitated, for as the latch noiselessly left its place, I felt I was given over to the execution of the task, whatever might be the results; to retreat now was impossible.

Silently I started to open the door. It swung well for a short distance, then the hinges began to squeak. Everything was quiet and my nerves were so wrought up, it seemed to me that the hinges were making noise enough to waken the household. I stopped pushing the door, and putting my ear to the opening, I could distinguish the regular breathing of the couple.

With this assurance, I persevered in opening the door in spite of the noisy hinges until I got a view of the interior of the room. Then I saw that the bed was one of the old style, with a high footboard, and was standing immediately in front of the door. The heads of the man and woman were in plain view. At the man's side was an old wooden chair on which stood the lighted candle. There also close to the candlestick lay a pair of formidable horse pistols. I could see everything but the baby, which was hidden somewhere on the other side of the high footboard.

While I was standing there, the man turned over restlessly, with his face away from the chair and the pistols. I reasoned it out that the child would be on the woman's side, because she was the one who would take care of it during the night. With this in mind, I stooped down, and under the shadow of the bedstead made my way on my hands and knees across the floor to the woman's side of the bed. As I was about to peer around the corner of the footboard, I heard the door close behind me. I certainly felt I was in a predicament shut in the room with a desperate man [and] a noisy woman, in search of someone else's baby. Being concealed by the high bed, I stopped long enough to look around and locate the door and its latch in case of trouble. There was nothing for me to do but to secure the baby and get away as quietly as I could.

Peeping around the foot of the bed, I saw a bundle lying close to the edge. Without waiting to see what it was, I dragged it toward me, and getting a firm hold pulled it off the bed. As I did there was a creak of the [bed]springs and the next moment the room was in darkness. There was no cause for secrecy now, so I jumped to my feet and rushed to the door. I heard the stool upset and the pistols fall. I heard the quick breathing of the man as he sprung out of bed and began feeling around on the floor in the dark for his weapons. Opening the door with a jerk, I ran across the kitchen out into the yard, with the bundle still in my arms. From their position in the room the man and woman saw me hurry out of the house, toward the road.

Confident of my success, they [my two adult fugitives] started toward the river. When I was within a few rods of them, I heard the crack of a pistol and a bullet went singing over my head. Instantly the two ahead of me swerved to one side of the road and started toward the cornfield. By this time I was opposite them and seeing their purpose, I called to them that I had the baby. The man said something about going back to the cabin and started in that direction with the woman after him.

There was no time to argue, seeing the two were about to desert me. I yelled as I went by them I had the baby, and if they wanted it, they would have to follow me. In a few minutes I heard the patter of their feet on the hard road as they came running after me. We soon reached the top of the riverbank.

There was a skiff at the landing, which I made the man turn loose, so that we could not be pursued. My own little craft was soon made ready, and I made the man lie down in the bottom of the boat, so that only two persons could be seen from the shore. Instead of going directly across, which would land me in front of my own house, I rowed up the river. I could see the other boat float down with the current, so that I felt there was no danger from that quarter.

We were about a third of the way across the river when we saw lights down at the landing which we had just left. We were still in plain sight, and I heard the voice of my employee shouting the name of the man in the bottom of the boat, warning him to come back. His threats fell on deaf ears, as I only increased my efforts to get across the river.

Arriving on the opposite side, I asked the man for my shoes, but much to my astonishment, he said that he had dropped them in his flight. They were a new pair of heavy shoes, coarse and different from what I was accustomed to wear. Still the shoes were a clue, and I was nervous as to how close the matter would come home to me. While I was provoked I could not stop to find fault, as the party had to be in hiding or out of town before morning.

Securing my skiff, we hurried up the bank to the home of my friend the attorney.[40] I only took time to tell him he must look after the fugitives, and then hastened home to prepare for the visit I expected would follow. Without striking a light I undressed and got into bed. It was not time to sleep, so I lay awake arranging my plans.

Soon I heard voices outside, then a loud knocking at the door. I was out of bed at the first sound, and throwing up the window I demanded who was making such a row. There were three men below, and the man who worked for me was spokesman. He was evidently surprised to find me, as he suspicioned me the first one, and expected I was away with the fugitives. In spite of finding me at home he began accusing me of running away his father's people. I protested.

"But you run them away," he cried. "No one but you would steal that baby."

"What baby?" was my response.

"You know all about that baby, and it is in your house."

Ordinarily I never permitted anyone to search my premises. This time I did not care, so I told them to wait while I put on my clothes, and I would come down and take the party through the house myself. This seemed to take them back completely, but I knew the longer I kept them busy with me the less likely they were to find their people. After consuming considerable time in dressing I went down.

The old man had his horse pistols in his hand, and he was mad clear through. I am sure if the old man had found his people in the house, he would have shot me down in cold blood. We went through the place room by room. They were completely crestfallen when the last corner was searched, and they failed to find their runaways. As the young fellow went out he turned and said, "I believe you were over the river just the same, and know where my people are."*

* *

The night's search was nothing compared to the scene I had when Srofe came into the shop the next morning dangling across his arm my new shoes, which had been dropped the night before by his runaway slave. He shoved the shoes in my

---

* At this point the Parker manuscript continues.

face, again declaring I had dropped them in getting his people
away. I just as stoutly denied the accusation. He had me scared
when he said he was going from store to store in the town
until he had the shoes identified.

While I put up a good bluff I . . . [did] try to beat him
uptown to tip off the merchant from whom I had purchased
the shoes on the previous day. All I could do was to hope and
pray that the merchant would not give me away. Srofe, true
to his word, did go from shoe shop to shoe shop, and not a
soul had ever seen the shoes before. Srofe hung around my
shop the rest of the day, but he never came back to work for
me. If he had only kept still, I would never have thought to
run his people off. But he put me on my mettle, so I rather
felt called upon to carry out the enterprise, to his own discom-
fiture.

ELEVEN

IT WOULD BE surprising for you to know that the little group of Ripley abolitionists came within an ace of anticipating John Brown's Raid at Harpers Ferry by several years.[41] It all seems so strange and unreal now. I wonder myself how we worked ourselves up to a pitch where it was only by the counsel of older and wiser men that the militant section was held back from undertaking the enterprise.

This was the way of it. One Sunday morning in midsummer, one of the Rankin boys came knocking on my door, arousing me from my sleep. It was after daylight, so I could see my visitor. He was very much excited and urged me to open the door immediately. Then unfolded the trouble. It seems that a group of five fugitives had either miscalculated the time or wandered from their route so that they arrived at the river just about daylight, too late to be ferried across. How the word got across the river to Rev. John Rankin I never did know, but he did receive the message, which started all the trouble.

Taking one of his boys, he immediately went to Tom Collins. Everything would have gone along in the normal way had not Rev. Rankin arrived at the Collins house after daylight and seen with his own eyes the group of fugitives standing at the water's edge on the Kentucky shore helplessly, and as it proved hopelessly, waiting for someone to rescue them.

Seeing the fugitives aroused Rev. Rankin to fever pitch of doing something to rescue the runaways. When I arrived at the Collins house, there was present in the front room Dr. Alexander Campbell, Eli Collins, Tom McCague, Rev. Rankin, and Dr. Beasley, who lived just across the street on the location now occupied by the home of Frank A. Stivers, the local banker.

They were gravely discussing the situation when I entered. I had been told to bring all my firearms, which I did, including an old musket. I knew something serious was up, because this was the first time I had ever been called on to come armed with anything but small arms.

I can still see the pale face of Rev. Rankin as he sat in the center of this council of war, arguing for his plan of rescue. I soon learned his plan was [to] take his six sons, myself, and any others who would join the expedition, go heavily armed in broad daylight, and take the group forcibly from anyone who got in the way. We knew that the lookouts on the Ohio side would make no move until the fugitives had landed on that side of the river.

As the reward for the capture and return of the slaves would amount to $1,000, which was more money than many of them had seen together in this lifetime, we felt they would conceal rather than reveal the presence of the runaways. This crowd would only become aggressive when we had them in charge, taking them through the town. The real menace on this Sunday was the discovery of the slaves by their owners or the Kentucky patrol, during the coming day. This is what Rev. Rankin and all the others were afraid would happen.

Once on this side of the river, the armed guard surrounding

the fugitives, mind you in broad daylight, would march up Mulberry Street to Fourth Street with the slaves, thence to the house of Rev. Rankin on top of the hill, where we would hold the fort until night, when we could secretly take them on their way to Canada. The question was, how would the citizens of the town take this invasion of an armed force into the friendly State of Kentucky?

Also, what would be the attitude [of] officers of the law? Furthermore, what would the angry Ohio patrol do at seeing their fugitives slipping through their fingers? What was still more menacing, would the Kentuckians invade Ohio and take by force their property?

This would bring on a pitch[ed] battle between the armed force in the Rankin house and the attackers from the outside. We [were] all familiar with an attack on the Rankins which had previously occurred when an all-day battle had been fought between Rev. Rankin and his sons on one side and mad Kentucky slave owners on the other side.

This affair was only ended when Rev. Rankin permitted William Harrison, a marble dealer, a citizen of Ripley, [to] search his house for the slaves, and report back to the attacking force that their people were not concealed in the house. As a matter of fact, they had been there and had been sent on during the night.

All these facts were brought forward by Dr. Campbell and Dr. Beasley, who were the most conservative and cautious members of the group. And it was to their wise counsel that we had in the end to submit. For a time the measure was in the balance, which indicates that there were other people who were thinking the same way John Brown was, except he went further and executed their ideas.

It was late in the morning before the council of war broke up. I am afraid I was disappointed, because I was sure the group would be captured before night. Rev. Rankin went to his church to preach. When he came to that part of his service that called for prayer, I was told afterwards by Tom McCague that the wrought-up preacher almost revealed the presence of the slaves and their serious situation in his appeal to the Almighty for their protection during the day. In fact, John Rankin himself told me that after his prayer he was sure that they would be watched over and protected.

It was a long day for all of us, and from time to time I looked across at the spot where I knew the fugitives were hiding to see if there was anything unusual happening. Early in the night, seven of us armed with muskets in a little flotilla of three boats, two occupied by the guard and one for the slaves, quietly rowed across the river to the spot where the people we were to rescue were seen. We found them all right, scared and hungry.

Just as quietly as we came, we stole away with the boat of fugitives between our boats. We landed at the foot of Mulberry Street [and] marched up the bank to meet face to face all the group who were at the meeting of the council of war. As for our program, we made no stop but [went] up Mulberry Street to the Rankin house, without being disturbed by the town or attacked by the law. Mrs. Rankin fed the hungry crowd.

After that there was no stopping until we delivered our charges at Red Oak Station of the Underground Railroad. That's how near the Ripley abolitionists came to anticipating John Brown and his Harpers Ferry adventure.

TWELVE

WHILE I AM on the subject of John Brown, I am reminded of the most important incident that ever took place at Ripley, during all the years of the activities of the abolition group. Strange as it may seem, no one placed any importance to the episode when it occurred, because we did not know what was in the mind of Harriet Beecher Stowe.[42] It was she who took the incident and wove it into the pages of *Uncle Tom's Cabin*, making it one of the most appealing and forceful attacks of this epoch-making book.

I am referring to that incident of Eliza with her babe in arms crossing on the ice, chased by dogs to the water's edge. This all really happened, and it took place at Ripley. I was not involved in this adventure, so I have to depend upon my friends who were and what I actually heard, though I did not know at the time what the trouble was.

I have the story directly from Rev. John Rankin, to whom Eliza told her story within an hour after she had made the crossing, as she sat by his fireside in his hilltop home.[43] Eliza was a young mulatto woman who lived back in Kentucky.[44] She was not married but her baby was ascribed to the overseer of the plantation. The day before her flight, a slave dealer had been in close conference with her master, which meant some of the slaves were being sold down the river, as Kentucky was a slave-breeding and not to any extent a slave-using state. This alarmed her to the point she decided she would run away with her baby, rather than be sent to the cotton fields, which had a bad reputation for treatment of slaves.[45]

Making her plans for escape, she left home early in the morning in midwinter, without any preparations for the journey or knowing how she would get across the river or to whom she was to apply for aid. In other words, she up and left, trusting to the future taking care of itself. How she stood the journey carrying her baby is still a mystery to me.

But she did it with a mother's determination and courage, arriving on the banks of the Ohio after dark, exhausted and driven to desperation by the cold. Seeing a light in a cabin, she took her chances, opened the door, and walked right into the arms of a white man. She was badly scared, but so utterly miserable she did not care what happened to her. Fortunately, the man was a gentleman living alone, and was not a slave owner.[46] Her condition so aroused the sympathy of the man he immediately made a place for her by his fire.

While she was thawing out [he] prepared food for her. While she ate, he accused her of being a runaway, which she freely confessed. Then he told her how helpless her case was; though the river was still frozen over, it had been thawing for several days and the ice was so rotten that no one dared go on, let alone attempt to cross on it.[47]

He further advised her to give herself up and go back home. She admitted she had about made up her mind to follow the . . . [gentleman's] advice when she heard the baying of the dogs, which she knew were on her trail. This made her so afraid she determined to go ahead and take her chances.

When the white man heard the dogs he became greatly agitated, again and again advising . . . Eliza to abandon her plans, which meant sure death. Seeing that she was determined to make the venture, the old fellow gave her a woolen shawl to put around her baby.[48] He then led the way out of his cabin towards the river. On the way he took a long wooden rail off the top of his fence, advising her that when she broke through the ice, the rail would catch on both sides of her, preventing her from being drowned. He then went back to his cabin, leaving her alone.

She had gotten down to the river's edge, stepped on soft ice, and went through. This made her stop and hesitate. As she was standing there trying to make up her mind [what] to do, the men and the dogs came down the bank at her, with such a rush she was forced to hurry on or be captured.

As she ran out on the ice the dogs were at her heels, but refused to go further. Strange as it may seem, the ice held until she disappeared in[to] the darkness. When the men came down the bank they yelled for her to come back and then began firing their pistols over her head. The sound of the bullets drove her on faster and faster until, coming to a weak spot, she went through the soft ice into the river. Throwing her baby from her, she clung fast to the rail, thus was prevented from sinking to the bottom of the river.

Scrambling out as best she could, she felt around in the darkness for her baby. She did not know what way she had thrown [it] in her desperate effort to save herself, [so] it was some time before she found it. All the while the dogs on the bank kept up a fearful noise, while the men were yelling and firing in her direction.

These unnerving things set her more determinedly on her way, until again she broke through the ice, and again she threw the baby from her, while she held on to the rail. Now cold, wet, and weary, she struggled out to find her baby and wearily continued her journey. A third time she broke through and a third time she had to go through the same efforts to secure her baby. This time she was so weak and exhausted, her clothes frozen to her body, she did not have the strength to even pull the rail along with her, so simply left to trust that the ice would hold, or else it would swallow her and her baby up.

The ice did hold until she reached the firm land. As she stepped off the shore ice onto the land, weary and disheartened, a caring hand came from some unknown source out of the dark and grabbed her. She told Rev. Rankin this was the last straw. She sank down on the ground and began to cry, feeling she was lost. Then the baby began to cry and a voice out of the darkness said, "Any woman who crossed that river, carrying her baby, has won her freedom."

It was Chance Shaw, one of the Ohio patrol.[49] Shaw now helped her to her feet [and], threw the wet shawl away, which the old gentleman had given her to protect the baby. Carrying the baby in his arms, he helped Eliza up the bank, guiding her through the streets of the town until he came in sight of the Rankin beacon light, which shone every night in the window. Pointing to the light, he told her if she would follow it she would find friends.

The first any of the Rankin household knew of the presence of Eliza was when Rev. John heard someone poking the fire in the sitting room. The door being always open to refugees, she made her way into the house and was poking the fire to warm her cold body and restore comfort to the baby. Later Rankin supplied dry clothes for mother and baby. While she sat by the fire, she told the story of the escape and crossing to Rev. Rankin . . .[50]

On the subject of Eliza, she [Harriet Beecher Stowe] had this to say: "Last spring while the author was in New York, a Presbyterian clergyman of Ohio came to me and said: 'I understand they dispute that fact about the woman's crossing the river. Now I know all about that; for I got the story from the very man that helped her up the bank. I know it is true, for she is now living in Canada.' "[51]

The Presbyterian minister we now know was Rev. John Rankin, as he was of that denomination. Furthermore, he was the only one that could know that Eliza had traveled to Canada over the Underground Railroad, of which he was an active conductor at that time. Rev. John Rankin did not dare confess his knowledge of Eliza openly; nor could Mrs. Harriet Beecher Stowe associate him with the crossing. If she had, he and his sons would have been sent to jail, their property confiscated.[52] So there was every reason why neither the minister [n]or Mrs. Stowe should openly declare his connection with the affair, nor specify Ripley as the point where the episode took place.[53]

THIRTEEN

THE SERIES OF incidents which I have related and am about to relate extended over a period of years, during which time I assisted 440 fugitives on their way to Canada.[54] For years I kept an accurate list of the names, dates, and original homes of the fugitives.

When the Fugitive Slave Law agitation was at its highest, and active prosecutions began its enforcement, everyone engaged in the work destroyed all existing evidence of his connection with it. My little memorandum book I dropped quietly in the cupola of my own iron foundry, so no one knew its existence, especially its damaging contents. But the work went on just the same, in fact, more aggressively than ever, which speaks well for the conscience and courage of the Ripley group.

As a result of my running off the Srofe slaves, the authorities of Mason County, Kentucky, offered a reward for me dead or alive. I had heard of this offer but placed little credence in the statement, until I read it myself, nailed securely to the bark of a tree.[55]

I had been up to Charleston Bottom arranging to aid a

group of slaves who were ready to start for Canada.[56] It was dark night. I had no fear of the road patrols, whose activities generally ceased long before midnight. So that as I went along the high road I saw a proclamation of some sort from time to time, never dreaming it related to me. They became so numerous my curiosity was aroused.

Striking a match I read in large letters: "REWARD $1,000 FOR JOHN PARKER, DEAD OR ALIVE." Not conducive to quiet one's nerves nor guarantee one's safety, particularly when I happened to be where anyone so minded could have had me, if they could catch or kill me. I did not go off whistling after I had read that sinister offer for my head, because I knew how deadly in earnest the men were who authorized billeting me from every fence corner as being worth $1,000 to any rascal who saw me.

However, the following week I was back at the Charleston Bottom, ready for the most humorous adventure of my career. It was a queer affair from the first and the further it advanced the [more] laughable it became, until its climax, which, in a way, was a tragedy to one of the slaves. I had made this appointment before I had read my own death warrant; but I decided to go on with it, since the runaways would be waiting for me to return. To my astonishment I found the slave quarters all dark, except one cabin which was very well lighted.

This unexpected situation caused me to stop and then advance cautiously to the lighted cabin to see what this illumination was about. It was like a scene from a comic opera I peered upon through a small window in the side of the cabin.

The room was filled with men and women and children, each one with a bundle. If they had left anything in the home or the house, it was because the utensil was too heavy to move or else it was nailed down. Tin pans, tin pails, and anything else that could make a racket were securely tied on the outside of the bundles. One woman had a footstool, another one her own favorite hoe. The other things in sight I had no desire to see or catalog.

What I did do was to wait and see if the row had aroused the suspicions of the master. When I felt assured on this point, I entered the cabin and blew out the lights myself. I made them put down their bundles. I then told the crowd that I could only take a few of them; the rest must bide their time until later.

Then the row started as each one grabbed his bundle, fairly arousing the dead with their noise and clamor. I couldn't get out of the door, so I went out through the window, across the fields like a scared rabbit to my boat, which I pushed off, thankful that I had not been captured and carted off to jail.

While I am on the humorous side of my otherwise tragic adventure, I must tell this little incident, which too had its scary side to one of its victims. I had been sent word that on a certain night on a certain plantation I would find a group of slaves ready to take the road, but there was no leader to show the way. Strange as it may seem, I had no hesitation in going to the rescue, in spite of the fact it might prove to be an ambush to capture me for the reward.

But I was there on time [and] I found a woman weighing 300 pounds who looked in bulk as large as an elephant. She was not of the original number, but having heard of the plan, had voluntarily joined the crowd, to their utter astonishment and fear. I told her she couldn't walk to the boat and if she did get there she would fill the boat herself. Nothing I could do or say affected her in the least. She was going along on the party, whether she could walk or not.

Knowing that she would yell her head off unless we took her, I happened to see a buggy in the yard. That settled the matter for the moment, so we lifted our fat lady into the buggy. I got into the shafts and started off with my crowd, determined in my own mind that the woman was not going along. I had to get rid of her so far away from the master's house her yelling could not be heard, but how?

A mud puddle settled the whole problem in a jiffy, for arriving in the midst of a soft spot, being a long distance from the house, I simply dropped the shafts of the buggy and ran away. The last I heard of my charge, she was yelling and screaming; how she got back to the house I never knew, but I landed my party safely and got them away so that they were never heard or seen again.[57]

A more serious aspect of this reward offered for me turned up in Cincinnati. As I suspected, the cupidity of some of the low whites was aroused by the offer of a fortune to them for me. I soon discovered that I was being watched and my every movement spied upon. They watched me, they watched my home, and kept tab on all those who called upon me. At a conference it was decided that until the matter of the reward quieted down, it would be safer for me to stay at home. Word was sent out that no fugitives were to be brought to my home. Furthermore I was not to pilot anyone along the road to freedom. So for a time I enjoyed seclusion and rest. This espionage kept up until I tired of it.

Once, just to test the mettle of my pursuers, I slipped out the back way, took a long aimless walk around town, [and] had the enjoyment of giving my spying friends a hope, which finally ended back home, having given myself and my watchful friends quite a bit of exercise.

But matters came to a head in an unexpected matter. It seems that Tom Collins had two parties of fugitives come to him the same night. The first party he took away as usual; the second party coming while he was away, someone in town, who did not know I was confined to my house, sent the second crowd to me. When they came to my door my wife answered the call out of the upstairs window.

While I could not see them, I felt they were genuine, and

badly in need of friendly assistance. I was soon ready for the road and prepared for anyone who attempted to interfere with me. The watchman was on my trail. I was determined to get rid of him one way or another, without kicking up too much of a disturbance.

Taking my time going up an alleyway that ran along the foundry, I hit upon my plan. Turning onto Second Street, I hung back in a shadow [and] waited for my man. He almost stumbled over me in his haste.

Grabbing him by the arm, I pushed him out into the moonlight so he could clearly see the knife which I held at his breast. I knew he was no coward, so I took no chances with him. Pressing my knife close to his chest, I told him I knew his Kentucky friends were paying to watch me, that I had enough of him and them, [and] unless he went on about his business, I would kill them at any other time I found him following me. It was his life or mine, this he knew, as I was in deadly earnest and meant exactly what I said. This was the end of the night watch.

The last serious effort to capture me for the reward led to an encounter and a real tragedy, which caused me much mental distress, and accusations for years after by the friends of the victim. I had been to Cincinnati on business and was returning on one of the large upriver packets, with no thoughts of trouble from any source. The steamer had hardly left the Cincinnati wharf when I ran into four Kentuckians, whom I had rather not met. Three of them were slave owners, whose slaves I had run away. The fourth man was a man by the name of Anderson, who lived in Dover, a Kentucky town a few miles below Ripley. While Anderson was not an avowed friend, I had done a good turn for him a short time previously, so I felt he was not my enemy. The other three Kentuckians were.

I was walking along the deck when I ran into this party of four men. One of them put his hand in his pocket, as if to draw a pistol. I was just as quick, cocking my pistol in my pocket, determined to fire through my coat if attacked. Anderson, who was really a quiet and peace-loving man, quieted down his belligerent friend, who turned away from me with a scowl. They had all been drinking and were in an ugly mood. There was trouble brewing and no one knew it better than I did.

On board of the steamer was a colored freeman from Ripley. He was a friend of mine but not a fighter, so I knew I could not depend upon him in case of an attack. But he could stand watch and he could keep me informed. Finding him on the lower deck, I induced him to come to my cabin.[58]

I then went to the captain, who was friendly to me, due entirely to the large amount of freight I gave his boat from my foundry. I told the captain of my encounter and told him I expected more trouble, which I wished to avoid. My plan was to retire to my cabin, and to keep to it until the boat reached Ripley.

For fear that both my friend and myself might fall asleep, I begged the captain to send someone to knock on the door to be sure we got off at Ripley. I implored the captain not to fail me, as the next stop after Ripley was Maysville, Kentucky; and if I were on board someone would be killed trying to drag me off the boat for the reward. Hearing the captain's assurance that I would be given ample notice in time to get off at our destination, I went back to my stateroom.

Having fallen asleep, for some unaccountable reason I awoke myself, [and] looked out the window to see the mouth of Eagle Creek, which was five miles past Ripley and halfway to Maysville. I had no time for recriminations against the captain. I was in serious trouble. I afterwards learned that the captain did send a porter to wake me, but the four men had prevented him from doing so, thus effectively trapping me, until they were ready to act on our arrival at Maysville.

Thinking I might get away, I opened my door on deck

quietly, only to see two of my enemies on watch. As my position was becoming more and more serious every minute, I opened the door leading in[to] the cabin, only to find the other two men on guard on that side. What to do was a problem, because I knew now that they had me in their hands and I was worth $1,000 to them dead. I knew that that was just what I might expect to occur.

Thinking they might let my friend, who was with me, through to see the captain, I explained to him the situation, and begged him to go see the captain and to have him land us on the Ohio shore, but the man was so badly scared he refused to do so. Then we were hopelessly trapped.

My companion made a suggestion which we finally decided to act upon, [even] if it led to killing anyone who got in our way. He said there was a yawl suspended over the stern of the boat, which could be lowered quickly in case of an emergency. Though it required three men to handle the lowering of the yawl, he thought the two of us could do so. Once safely in the water, we could row back to Ripley, and the steamer could pick up her boat on her next trip back to Cincinnati. It was such a feasible plan, I fell in with [it at] once. Having a plan and only a short time to execute it, there was no time to lose. Knowing my companion and knowing myself, I took his pistol, determined to act as bodyguard while he handled the lowering of the yawl. There was only one way to get by the man guarding our door, and that was to start shooting as soon as I got out the door.

Placing my companion behind me, I opened the door and stepped out on the deck with a pistol in each hand, only to find my guard gone. Beckoning my companion, I started on the run for the stern of the boat, determined to shoot down any one of my would-be captors. Much to my surprise there was not a soul in sight. While I stood guard my comrade swung over the water into the yawl.

Everything seemed to be working to our advantage. My

friend had loosened the front guy rope and was working at the stern guy rope of the yawl. I was reaching for the rope to swing over into the yawl when two of my enemies came thundering down the deck with pistols in hand. I opened the encounter by firing point-blank at one, who fell to the deck, then exchanged shots with the other one, until he dodged into a cabin.

Backing away to where the loose end of the yawl rope lay, I swung myself into the bow in the still suspended yawl where my companion was struggling with the stern line holding the yawl. The steamer was under full way; I could see the eddying water bubbling up from beneath her hull at least 20 feet below me.

Dropping the pistol I had discharged into the bottom of the boat [and] putting the other one in my pocket, I began working desperately at the line that held the bow of the yawl. My comrade was equally as busy, but both of us being ignorant in the method of launching the yawl, made little progress. There was a hitch somewhere, but I knew nothing about the rigging, so there we hung in midair, the yawl swaying back and forth, threatening at any time to throw both of us into the boiling water below us. We tugged, strained, and pulled at the ropes, in a last frantic effort for our release.

What happened I never knew, for the next thing I knew, the yawl was flying through the air, and the next instant struck the water with a jerk that threw me overboard. Flailing out frantically, I was fortunate enough to seize the side of the yawl, which was still attached to the steamer, dragging behind it in a half-submerged condition. When I had regained my senses, I looked around for my companion, but he was gone, and I never saw him again.

My position now was worse than when I was on the deck of the steamer, for in my haste I had neglected unfastening the rope that held the yawl to the steamer. The result was that the yawl, to which I was holding, was bouncing up and down, and at the same time was being dragged through the water at great speed. The rope tied to the steamer pulled the bow of the boat high out of the water, but sunk the side to which I was clinging, so that half the time my head was under water.

The long rope gave the yawl so much play, it swung into the waves from the paddle wheels, threatening to tear me loose and set me afloat down the river. My situation seemed hopeless, for if let loose, my clothes would pull me down; if I stayed where I was, I was a helpless target for my enemies, who I knew would soon find me. All I thought of at the time was how long would it be before I would be shot. I have no recollection of having fear of drowning, so I clung desperately to the side of the leaping yawl.

My head bobbed under the water one moment, when all seemed over. The next moment, looking blearily through the water dripping . . . over my eyes, I saw the form of a man on the deck high over my head. Then I knew my end had come.

But I held on just the same, determined to fight, [trusting in] my good luck to the end of the game of chase I was then so hopelessly playing. I had expected the shooting to commence at once, and pulled myself together to prepare for the shock. My face being up longer this time, I saw the man was Anderson and he had no pistol. He was the only man that might show some compassion on me.

If ever a man threw his trembling soul into an appeal, I did as I pleaded with Anderson. He made no response to my appeal and stood heartlessly watching me as I helplessly rose and sank with the half-submerged yawl. I yelled to him for God sake cut the rope, but my begging fell upon deaf ears, as he soon turned away and left me to my fate.

My heart grew faint and my grip on the yawl weakened, as I felt my position was hopeless and I was only prolonging the agony. It was my obsession against drowning that called me to my task. I was too much of a fatalist to ever fear death, when my time came, I would go, but I was afraid of drowning. It was a last minute of holding on that prevented me from slipping away.

In the twilight I saw a man. Then the yawl seemed to sink away from the steamer. Anderson had cut the rope. Once I ceased to be hauled relentlessly by the steamer, the yawl settled to an even keel. It was easy then for me to scramble over the side of the little boat and sink down helplessly into the water with which it was partially filled. I floated downstream oblivious to my surroundings until I was aroused by the feeling that the yawl had gone ashore.

Arousing myself from my exhausted stupor, I stirred myself to activity when I discovered I was hard aground in Kentucky, that last place I wanted to be. As the oars had been lost, I pulled off a slat. Using it as a paddle, I slowly and painfully made my way to the Ohio shore and safety.

My comrade's body was found several days later, with a bruise on the side of the head, evidently made by striking the yawl as he was thrown overboard. He was known to be an excellent swimmer. My enemies made the most of this fact— accused me of killing him, and made every effort to have me indicted for murder. It merely indicates how desperate were the men to trump up any charge in order to get me permanently out of the way.

FOURTEEN

WHEN I FIRST began my work among the slaves, all northern Kentucky was still covered with virgin forest, broken here and there by clearings, with many trails and few roads. But the prime bluegrass regions were thickly settled and rich in money and slaves. As the settlers began to build their cabins and make their clearings, the forest gradually disappeared. The increased population made it more difficult for the fugitives to pass through the country successfully, since there were many eyes to watch and few hiding places to conceal.

Another disadvantage was the gradual reduction in the number of slaves in the Borderland. This was due to two causes; so many slaves ran away, their owners, fearful of loss, sold the slaves down the river. As the fugitive depended entirely on his own race for assistance, this removal of his own people increased his difficulties of getting food and directions.

But these obstacles did not deter those slaves who were intelligent and determined to break away from their bondage. The early fall was the time that most of them selected to strike out for themselves. Though the warm summer nights were preferable for comfort, sad experiences had taught him that it was the cornfield on which he must depend for food. Besides, the ground was hard and difficult to track in the autumn.

Frequently they told me that they would wait weeks, after they had decided to run away, waiting for the corn to ripen. As soon as this food supply [was available] they were off. They always started with a bag of provisions and a load of unnecessary things. These were thrown away, until he got down to his knapsack of food.

Men and women whom I helped on their way came from Tennessee, requiring weeks to make the journey, sleeping under the trees in the daytime and slowly picking their dangerous way at night. How they crossed the numerous creeks that lay waiting for them like a trap was unbelievable to me. As a matter of fact, they became backwoodsmen, following the north star, or even mountains, to reach their destination, the Ohio River. Once there they felt they were in view of their promised land, even if they had no way to cross into it. Few had shoes, and these were so worn out by the time they reached me, the soles were held together by twine—making loose-fitting sandals.

These long-distance travelers were usually people strong physically, as well as people of character, and were resourceful when confronted with trouble, otherwise they could have never escaped. The riffraff runaways came from the Borderland, where it was comparatively easy to get away and they were not tested by repeated risks. Some of them were difficult to control.

I had an experience with one of these uncontrollable groups which made me very chary about my fugitives ever after. To begin with, they were stranded on the Kentucky shore, when I appeared rowing slowly along the shore with no object in view. My attention was attracted to them by their talking loud enough for me to know they were colored folks, and their position indicated they were runaways. Landing, I found them with ease and offered my services to get them across the river.

They were suspicious of me, and hesitated until I told them frankly they could go or stay and be captured, before they would go with me. I took them to the home of Tom McCague and concealed them in the hay. They became so noisy before I left them I decided to take them to the house and hide them in his garret.

There they became so noisy Tom McCague sent for me to quiet the lot. It was dark in the garret; [that] was what they were complaining about. I was so mad at their stupidity, one of the men making some slighting remark. I gave him a sound thrashing, and after that the crowd were meek and mild. I never had anything to do with such a rowdy crowd, and was glad to get rid of them as soon as it was dark.

In strong contrast to this shiftlessness and ingratitude of the group of rowdy fugitives, which I have just narrated, was the courage and resourcefulness of a couple of slaves who came to me from southern Kentucky. For some reason these slaves, failing to secure proper directions, had fallen into the hands of a paid spy who was en route to the town marshal's office when the party was overtaken by colored freemen, who forcibly rescued the two fugitives and brought them to my house, which was not only thoughtless, but dangerous to me.

As it was too late to get them away before daylight, I did the second wrong thing by hiding them in my own house, something which I had always refused to do before. So I took them up to my attic, hoping that there was no one [who had] followed the fugitives to my house. Then the rumpus began and I had the fright of my whole life.

For it seems that after the rescue, the Ripley spy met an armed crowd from across the river in pursuit of their own run-aways. While the two slaves in my attic were not their property, the party thought this was their one chance to get even if not completely rid of me as a menace to their own slaves.

They evidently knew I had received the two men, for I had hardly settled myself down for a nap when there came a hard knocking at my front door. I made the third mistake this night by going directly to my door instead of making my first observations out of the front window. As I unlocked and opened the door the crowd rushed me, seizing me violently.

They were quite forward in their telling me that I had finally been caught in their own trap. They furthermore informed me that two slaves had been seen entering my house, and that they were still concealed somewhere within its four walls, and they proposed to search the house until they found them.

Being helpless in their hands, I made a great bluff of innocence, asking them to search the house, if they wished to do so. They would have done it without my consent, so I made the best of a bad situation, trusting to my resourcefulness to get me out of the trouble. As you will see, it was wise tactics on my part.

First they examined every nook and corner downstairs, placing guards around the house to see that no one got away. Not having formulated a plan, I delayed the search as much as I could, still looking for a loophole. Having finished the first floor, they started up the stairs, when I brought them back to examine a closet which had been overlooked, thus working every conceivable delay to gain time.

At the top of the stairs I shouted in a loud voice to my captors that they could look the house over and even on the roof, [but] they would find no one. This I did for the benefit of the two slaves in the attic, not only to notify them of their danger, but to give them a clue to take refuge on the roof, which was my only chance of getting out of the jam. After this loud talk I conducted the party into my bedroom, kept them busy looking into closets, slamming the doors, and making all the confusion I could, to muffle any row the slaves might make in their efforts to escape capture.

My captors were in no mood to delay matters, feeling sure of finding their prey, then, not finding them as they went from room to room, they became angry and abusive. They also interpreted all my forwardness in helping their search was in an effort to divert them from the real place of concealment.

They then took matters into their own hands and brooked no further interference. I made no complaint, because I knew my men had ample time to do what they were able to in carrying out their plans of concealment or escape, neither of which I was exceedingly doubtful could be done.

All the while I was fairly quaking inwardly with fear, from the discovery of the two slaves that would surely follow when the garret was searched. I put off swallowing this bitter pill as long as I could, as I could see the confiscation of all my land and seized property, and the wreckage of my whole life's work. I had a fleeting hope that in some way the stairs to the attic would be overlooked, as the whole party had passed by them in their search.

It was only a fleeting hope, however, for as we crowded out into the hall one of the searchers exclaimed: "There's the attic stairs." If the man had pronounced the judgment of death upon me, I could not have felt the shock more than I did at this announcement of his discovery.

As we climbed the stairs one at a time I thought it would be best for the slaves as well as myself to confess my guilt, call on the two men to surrender, and thus put an end to my manhunt. Then I calmed down, stood fast on my section of landing on to the last minute and beyond, and held my breath.

I knew the room permitted no hiding place for one man, let alone two, as it was a plain attic with rafters showing overhead and clear floor beneath. The detection of the two men was only a question of a few moments. The man ahead of me carried a lighted lantern, the feeble rays dimly dispelling the darkness of the attic. Looking through the gloom, I saw the shadowy outline of the two . . . figures in the farthest corner.

I faltered and my heart went sick as I waited for the exultant shout of the men about me. If the leader was blind, surely the men who crowded up the stairs would see, but they too stared and said nothing. Could my eyes deceive me? Not at all, because there in front of them I could see the two fugitives, so that it was only a question of time for my captors to be accustomed to the surrounding darkness, to see the slaves as I saw them.

I turned my eyes away, for fear my staring would give the position of the two slaves away. Still I could not conceive how two men could be in plain sight as these were to me, and not be seen by the rest of the party. I suggested that we go back downstairs. Instead, the man with a lantern advanced further into the attic, while the outline of the two fugitives faded away, leaving only an empty space.

A diligent search throughout the garret proved that the men had escaped, [a surprise] to me and a complete puzzle to the searchers. I was really puzzled myself until I discovered the ladder leading to the roof was missing. Then it was that I knew that my two men were hugging the roof, but they had [taken] the precaution to haul up the ladder with them. I had a bad moment when the man with the lantern held it high over his head; it was only the last act of his futile search of the disappointed crowd.

Before leaving they swore unless they found the men, they would return the next night and burn my home. While it was an idle threat, it did indicate to me that they were not satisfied I did not have the two men hid away someplace in my home. It also warned me I must be careful in getting my men away the following night. It was well that I took heed, as you will soon see.

After due allowance of time and also examination, I succeeded in getting the two men down from their precarious position on a slanting roof and hid them in my cellar during the following day. Expecting a visit from my captors of the previous night, I decided to get them out of my house as soon as it was dark, and furthermore I would not guide them out of town, but would assign this task to Tom Collins, who would not be watched.

Without waiting for the people of the town to quiet down, I led the two fugitives along Front Street to the home of Collins. As we entered I saw a man in a shadow, whom I knew was on watch, and we had been discovered. There was no time to lose. In the hurried conference with Collins, we decided his house was not safe and the only available space was in his workshop in his back yard.

We had hardly reached the shop when there was hard knocking at the front door. Then a second and a third impatient and threatening pounding which threatened to force the door from its hinges. Finally Collins, having hurriedly reentered his house, opened the door, dreading the cause of so much violence.

He was faced by the same crowd that had visited my house the night before, and greeted by the statement that he was harboring runaways, who had been seen to enter his house a short time before. Without arguing the point he invited them to enter and search his house, depending on me to take care of the fugitives.

Suspecting that the house was watched on all sides, I slid out the back way through a vacant lot, only to find a man on guard. Fortunately he did not see me. Returning to the shop, I advised the men it was a case of fighting our way through the group of slave owners or overcoming the guard, which I had made up my mind to do, when I was startled to hear voices in the yard headed towards the shop, completely blocking my way out to the alley. Hastily looking around the shop, all I could see was a carpenter's bench and old cupboard, both of which were out of the question as places of concealment.

Lying along the floor in a row were a number of coffins, ready for use. Fortunately, the tops lay on the caskets loosely. Picking up one lid, I motioned a man to get in. He hesitated until I pushed him and placed [the] lid on top of him. The second man I concealed in the same manner. The third casket I selected for myself.

While it has taken time to tell of our actions, I assure you it only took a breath or two to execute them. I let the silence of the shop bear out its grim prospects. We did not have long to wait in our places of self-internment until the crowd trooped into the shop. Though they examined the shop, and cupboard particularly, they did not in that gloom care to touch the row of coffins, feeling assured that no colored man would ever consign his living body to such a place of concealment.

Fortunately, this superstition prevailed. I almost coughed, and I was afraid one of the other men might not be able to control himself as well as I had done. However, the fortunes of war were with us, and the searchers, standing around for a few minutes discussing our disappearance, left the shop apparently to go away.

I stayed in my coffin until my nerves began to jump, then I pushed aside the lid and stepped out of my gruesome hiding place. The two fugitives were as much affected by the coffins as I was, in fact they were more fearful of them than they were of the presence of their enemies. I assure you that if the pursuers had returned, I do not believe I could have persuaded them to return to their caskets.

After waiting until I thought the excitement was all over, I gradually opened the door, only to look into the face of a man who was standing by for us to come back. Leaping back, I drew my pistol and waited.

While I was standing there fearful and expectant of trouble, there was a gentle tap. Then it came to me that my man was Tom Collins with a message. Opening the door slightly, he told me that the house was guarded in front and the alley as well. He did not tarry, but left me with the two charges on my hands. What was I to do? It was evident I could not stop there.

As the front and rear of the Collins house was watched, the only way out was over the side fence through the neighboring yards. Fortunately, my friend and colleague Tom McCague lived a few yards away, so it was only a matter of care and caution to go cross yards to find a safe refuge with him.

This I did, leading the way with my two men following me like two moving shadows. Making my way into the house, I soon had him up, my story told, and the two men left in his care while the would-be watchers kept their silent but hapless vigil.

After carefully surveying the field, I went over more back fences and more lots until I came to another alley, which I followed down to Front Street, thence back home, having finally gotten rid of the two most perplexing fugitives I ever had anything to do with. They went to Canada the next night, with someone else as guide. . . .

FIFTEEN

EVEN MY ADVENTURES of comedy had a way of trailing off into the tragic, which made me keep my wits keen to what was going on about me. This next incident was the final one, so far as I knew, that had to do with the seeing of that $1,000 reward, which in those days was large enough to induce my would-be captors to take the greatest chances.

That I survived was due not so much to bravery or courage but to a second instinct of suspicion and trouble. I might also say to the crude way that the men engaged in the enterprise approached me. It was poor planning and worse thinking that was my real safety.

Of course, I was never off guard myself, while my wife was a good watchdog herself. As my home was on the top of the bank of the river, it was easy of access to anyone who cared to row across the river and walk up to the top of the bank. Besides, my house was remote from my friends, which made it all the more accessible to those who ventured to attack me. It was so easy to reach, one night a band of kidnappers made the venture; as you can surmise from my opening words, with the tables turned to humor rather than the reward. So it did open, but in the end, well, that's the story.

I was aroused about midnight by gentle rapping on my front door, as I kept it locked and chained so that no one could enter. It was one of those timid pleading knocks which would indicate runaways uncertain of their position and badly scared. As usual my wife did the preliminaries by throwing up the window, while I stood beside her to size up the situation. There was a single colored man standing at the door. I asked him what he wanted. To my query he replied that he was a runaway, and for me to come down at once.

My wife, who, of course, had heard the conversation, intuitively mistrusted the man—accordingly advised me strongly not to go down. From the man's speech I knew he was a colored man, and I felt might be in distress. In spite of my wife's warnings I went down. Placing the chain in position, I stood out of sight.

Instead of coming to the top step where I could see him, he persisted in standing away on the ground, insisting on my coming out, instead [of] begging me to let him in. Now I was on guard, suspecting a trick of some sort was about to be worked on me.

The man had a perfectly earnest story in that he had run away to Canada leaving his wife behind. He had now come back for her and wanted me to go with him to her rescue. I told him it was too late to try tonight, but if he would come in and spend the day with me, we would go the next night. To this he replied we must go that night as his wife was to be sold the next day. This statement I did not believe, because I knew under the circumstances no return slave would have such advance and accurate information.

By this time I had my plans to get him into the house, so I could make him tell me the truth. Standing behind my chained door, I began sympathizing with him at the possibility of the loss of his wife, and invited him to come to the top step, where I could speak with him freely. After some talk I finally persuaded him to come up to the doorway.

In the meantime, I had slipped the door chain, and was ready for action. As the man reached the top step, I suddenly threw the door wide open, reached out and grabbed him by the coat collar. With a quick jerk I drew him into the house, and slammed the door, chaining and locking it. I had my man now at close quarters.

In the meantime, my wife, who had been standing at the top of the stairs, came down with a lighted lamp, so I could get a good look at my captive. He was a stranger to both of us. There was no question as to his color, as he was black as ebony. I began questioning the man, and the more he talked, the more I was convinced there was something radically wrong with his story and himself.

Next door to me lived one of my best molders. He was a white man, loyal to me and sympathetic with my work among the slaves. I sent my wife over to bring Tim, as I felt there was work for two of us, to get the truth out of my man.[59]

When Tim came I told him of my suspicions. Tim went after the man roughshod, threatening to throw him in the cupola unless he came out with the truth. The man began to grow weary, and said he did not want to lose any more time, but would go by himself to rescue his wife; at the same time [he] edged towards the door. I blocked the way, pointing my revolver at the man.

I told him that unless he told me the truth I would shoot him. This was too much for the black man, as he fell to his knees [and] begged for his life. He then confessed he was only a decoy, sent by four men who were all strangers who came from back in Kentucky, [who] were lying behind a log on the riverbank waiting for him to bring me down to the skiff.

He said that the men planned to kidnap me, if I resisted, to kill me. They were determined to earn the reward of $1,000 dead or alive. He pleaded he was there against his will, as one of the men was his master, and had threatened to kill him if he had not come and told the story he did. Strange as it may seem, the man pleaded for me to turn him loose so he could go back to his master. Tim was for giving the fellow a good beating and sending him back to his treacherous master.

As I was standing with my back to the door, watching my man in dim lamplight, the thought came to me of running the slave off to Canada, as a good joke on his master. When I unfolded my story to Tim, the slave pleaded he did not want to go to Canada and leave his wife. He promised faithfully he would come back the next night if we would only let him go now.

Tim looked at me, but I shook my head and said we would run him away whether [he wished it] or no. The man begged and pleaded, but I was more interested now in sending a warning on [to] my enemies than I was in the wishes of this man. As I could not go myself, I told Tim to take him to Red Oak and leave him. With pistol drawn, Tim and the man went on their way. The last I saw of the slave was the Irishman close on his back swearing dire threats unless he went along peaceably to Canada.

With the decoy gone, I foolishly determined to seek my would-be kidnappers in their wooden log lair. By this time it was getting towards daylight as it was in July. I decided to give Tim a good lead, so I waited as long as I could before I began my performance. Having waited [until] the last minute, placing two pistols in my jacket, carrying my hunting knife openly in my hand, with a large English mastiff at my heels, I started over the bank to confront my enemies.

Being thoroughly familiar with the ground and the log back of which the men were lying, I was careful to approach them

from the river side between them and their skiff, which I saw
drawn up on the shore. Coming opposite the log, I drew my
pistol and called for the men to come out. As there was no
answer, for a moment the thought came to my mind perhaps
the slave had deceived me. All such notions left me when I
saw the gleam of a gun over the top of the log. I needed no
further evidence to establish the sinister ambush that had been
prepared for me.

A second time I called the men, warning them that I knew
of their hiding place. Furthermore I had summoned my
friends, who were at the top of the bank, ready to shoot them
down if any injury came to me. Of course, the only force present was myself, my wife, and my dog. The only response to
this statement was the ominous click of a rifle as it was cocked,
made ready to fire. My faithful dog came to my rescue as he
now leaped on the top of the log and began barking furiously.

This diversion no doubt saved my life, for the four men,
seeing their hiding place was known, now came out in the
open and confronted me. They were armed with rifles and pistols in their belts, as the dawn now began to break over the
eastern hills. They were threatening and furious, demanding
their slave. I was perfectly oblivious of any man and demanded
to whom they referred, what was his name, and where was
he going.

My calm defiance only irritated them the more until they
turned on me and threatened, unless I produced their man
immediately, they would shoot me on the spot. I am quite
sure it never occurred to them that their man was gone at this
time, [for had they realized it] they would have shot me
offhand.

As they persisted in wanting to know where their man was,
I kept asking, "What man?" determined to force a confession
out of their own perfidy. Finally one of the men confessed they
had sent a man to my house. I replied there was a runaway at

my house who wanted to go to Canada, and the last I saw of him he was going that way.

Then my good fortune shone on me, and I assure you I needed it badly. For as the men were drawn up ready to shoot me, a neighbor whom my wife had aroused called me by name from the top of the bank. I answered, saying I was talking to four men, giving their names, saying I was coming at once. Backing away from the party, I kept my face toward them, as I did not propose to be shot down without defending myself.

I backed away, until I reached a point of safety, leaving four men standing helplessly by with a hatred that but for their own safety would have prompted them to shoot me down in my tracks. Once out of the range of their guns, I was rightly glad to run as fast as I could to safety. From the top of the bank I saw the skiff with the four men pull away, fairly beside themselves with rage, and one of them less a slave for their futile night's raid.

I was anxious about the slave whom I was forcibly running away, because all he had to do was to raise an outcry and the law would be back of him. But Tim reported that the man decided that it was too good a chance to lose, and agreed to go on via the Underground Railway. So far as I ever knew he must have reached his promised land.

Afterword

THE ORIGIN OF this book and the saving of the John Parker house in Ripley, Ohio, are due to the efforts of Charles Nuckolls and Robert Newman, who began on quite separate paths and then found out about each other, combined their efforts, and found a friendship as well.

Charles Nuckolls was born in Ashland, Kentucky, a few miles upstream on the Ohio River from Ripley. The son of two high-school teachers, he became a teacher and principal after receiving his master's degree in history from the Ohio State University. When he learned of the John Parker house in the spring of 1993, and its state of near collapse, Nuckolls attempted to purchase it with the help of his brothers. When the house's historical value became known, the price was raised beyond Nuckolls's means. Yet he persisted in the attempt to raise the necessary funds.

Robert Newman is a civil-rights attorney in Cincinnati. Some of Newman's successful cases include *Crow v. Brown*, the public-housing desegregation case in Atlanta; *Kahles v. Luken*, the workhouse closure case in Cincinnati; and *Dunn v. Voinovich*, a statewide class-action suit on behalf of all mentally ill inmates in the Ohio prison system. Newman's resume also includes several important cases that were unsuccessful, including *Wine v. Staples,* an attempt to increase the level of welfare benefits in Ohio, and *Avery v. Jennings,* an attempt to end political patronage in governmental hiring in Ohio.

Newman's first acquaintance with John Parker's name came by accident, while he was researching and writing a paper on John Rankin, an early abolitionist who had moved to Ripley after being asked to leave Kentucky for teaching blacks to read. A footnote in a doctoral dissertation identified John Parker as a collaborator with Rankin in the underground railroad. Newman located and obtained a copy of the handwritten Gregg manuscript from the Duke University Library. Over the course of several nights, he read the barely legible manuscript. He trembled with excitement, he said, as the story unfolded.

When Newman learned of Nuckolls's unsuccessful efforts to purchase the Parker house, the two joined forces, hoping that Parker's own manuscript could be used to finance the purchase of his house.

The proceeds from this book have made that dream possible. The royalties from *His Promised Land* go directly to the John P. Parker Historical Society, in the hopes of restoring and commemorating the life of John Parker, his role in the underground railroad, and Parker's "personal war against slavery."

ACKNOWLEDGMENTS

THE JOHN P. PARKER Historical Society would like to thank many of those who have helped save the Parker House and who have helped publish the Parker story: Theresa McGoron, Beth Wells, and Sue Daczko who typed the manuscript; David Hamilton Peck, Esq.; David Hendin, our friend and agent; Amy Cherry, our editor; Paul Knue, who gave us good ideas; Bruce Goetzman, our architect friend; and all the good people in Ripley who have stuck with us through thick and thin—Betty Campbell, Miriam Zachman, Tom Zachman, Carol Stivers, John Cooper, James Settles, Mary Ann Brown-Olding, The Village Council, and the Ripley banks who loaned us money in the nick of time. We gratefully acknowledge The Special Collections Library at Duke University for their assistance in the publication of *His Promised Land*.

Notes

PREFACE BY STUART SEELY SPRAGUE

1. Information about Parker is scant. For example, we are forced to fall back on the Gregg manuscript to determine which parent was African-American and which Caucasian and for his activities prior to moving to Ripley. Where they exist, corroborating sources, including censuses and city directories, have been used. No clearly identifiable photograph of John P. Parker is known to exist. Thanks to Alison J. Gibson of Ripley's Union Township Public Library and Michel S. Perdreau of Athens, Ohio who graciously shared sources, and to Jerry Gore of Maysville who first alerted me to the Parker manuscript.

2. There is little in print about John P. Parker. A brief biographical sketch appears in the 1883 *History of Brown County*. Henry E. Baker included Parker in his 1917 *Journal of Negro History* article "The Negro in the Field of Invention," and Frank R. Levstik wrote the Parker entry in Logan and Winston's *Dictionary of Negro Biography*.

Only in recent years have historians paid attention to Parker. The first substantial article came out in *Ohio History* (1971) with Louis Weeks's "John P. Parker: Black Abolitionist Entrepreneur, 1827–1900." That article includes liberal excerpts from the memoir. Paul Young has published two articles in *Ohio Southland*, "John Parker: Ripley's Black Abolitionist" (Winter 1990) and "The Underground

Railroad" (Issue #1, 1991). Edith M. Gaines's *Freedom Light: Underground Railroad Stories from Ripley, Ohio* (1991) spotlights Parker as well as Rankin. Parker was also featured in John Cooper's "Restoring History," *River Hills* (Summer 1994).

3. By going through the annual *Catalog of Officers and Students at Yale University* for the years in which the doctor's sons headed north to study, I hoped to identify the doctor since students' hometowns were listed. I compared the Yale surnames with the Mobile city directory to identify the doctor, but found no appropriate match. It is possible the two sons failed entrance exams or decided they did not like Connecticut and returned.

4. Gist's slaves arrived in June 1818 and set up two "camps," known as the upper and lower camp. Because of the poor quality of the land and the better opportunities available working on steamboats, the two African-American settlements never prospered. In 1837 a school was set up, but the schoolhouse was burned down. An article in the *Cincinnati Whig* written in 1836 exemplifies the racism of the time: "Farms given to them 15 years ago instead of being well improved, and timber preserved for farming have been sadly managed. . . . They are so excessively lazy and stupid that the people of Georgetown (near their camps) and neighboring farmers will not employ them." The Gist slaves were not the only ones who were emancipated and settled in Brown County. The Rev. Samuel Doak also freed his slaves in 1818, and eleven came to Brown County.

5. Many of the slaves John Parker rowed across the Ohio River were forwarded on to Red Oak, where a large number of families willingly took in fugitives.

6. Information regarding Parker's businesses is from the R. G. Dun & Co. Collection, Baker Library, Harvard University Graduate School of Business, Ohio volume 17, pp. 240, 344, 424, 442. The credit-rating agency depended upon responsible community leaders to evaluate the creditworthiness and character of individual businessmen and their firms. Those who provided the confidential information are identified by number, not by name.

Of Alfred Belchamber, with whom Parker was involved in the threshing-machine-making business, an informative letter from Eb McKinley to Isaac Addison McKinley dated Ripley, April 30, 1859, declares that "he is a very clever, industrious merchant of good moral habits. He builds threshing machines of his own getting up; a combination of several of the best machines in use. He is now gone on a tour of Kentucky, to put up a new hemp break that he has just finished and will be absent a few days." Cincinnati Historical Society, C. M. Carson Collection.

7. St. Paul, Minnesota *Appeal,* February 14, 1891.

8. By the 1920s, Parker's Phoenix Foundry became the Ripley Foundry and Machine Company. Wilbur H. Siebert in *Ripley* (Ohio) *Bee,* June 17, 1948, copy in the Wilbur H. Siebert Collection, Box 115, Ohio Miscellaneous, Ohio Historical Society, Columbus, Ohio. Siebert was interested primarily in agents of the Underground Railroad who forwarded fugitives toward Canada, which may explain why there is no surviving contemporary evidence of the interview. There are notes regarding the three other Ripley, Ohio, interviews of that day.

9. The dates of birth for Portia and Bianca are derived from their ages given in censuses of Brown County, Ohio.

10. Gregg (1864–1937) was the son of Samuel Gregg, a dry goods merchant and Martha (McCracken) Gregg. After graduating from high school in Ripley, he headed out to Colorado, where he became a section hand on the Union Pacific Railroad. From there he went to Chattanooga, Tennessee, where he worked for three years in a candy factory. Then he became a reporter with the Chattanooga *News.* It may have been during his years with the *News* that he returned to Ripley to interview Parker. Circumstantial evidence supporting this view includes references to Parker as "an old man," to Gregg's reputation as a journalist, and to Parker's residence, which was destroyed by fire in 1889 but is mentioned as being intact in the manuscript. 1886–1889 is the most likely time frame for the interview.

Gregg left the *News* for the *Cleveland* (Ohio) *Press,* where he worked for five years. He married and became an active member of Cleveland's business community. He organized the Cleveland Street Lighting Company, purchased in 1906 the Cleveland Macaroni Company, and became president of the Cleveland Worm and Gear Company.

His affection for Ripley combined with his wealth led him to organize the 1912 Centennial Celebration of Ripley; he purchased bronze plaques to be installed in front of historic houses and bought the "Liberty Monument," which was unveiled as part of the centennial. I suspect he was also responsible for the May 1910 photographing of Parker's house, of the African-American church, and of other African-American places. Gregg was an amateur historian, publishing *Andrews' Raiders* (1891), *The Founding of a Nation* (1915), and *Voice of the Nation and Other Verses* (1918). His "Anti-Slavery Notes," a transcription of historical source works, can be dated from his home address to 1907 while "The Borderland" is dated 1908. Both are at the Ohio Historical Society.

In a fragment of Gregg's never published "The Imperial Forest," he wrote of Parker, "I remember going through his library in after years and was astounded at its quality of philosophy, history, poetry and drama, but there was no fiction. He had become a highly educated man through his books."

11. Following the 1850 Fugitive Slave Law a number of Indiana slavenappers who had helped slaves escape from Kentucky were arrested and taken back to Kentucky. For such crimes, prison sentences of 5–20 years were common.

12. James West Davidson and Mark Hamilton Lytle, *After the Fact: the Art of Historical Detection* 3rd edition (New York, 1992), "The View From the Bottom Rail," 148–177.

13. Three manuscripts, John Rankin's Autobiography, which may have been used in a disjointed 26 part serial that the Emporia, Kansas *News* ran during 1874–75, the Parker Memoir, and the "Eliza" manuscript comprise Duke University's Rankin-Parker Collection. No source is given for the donor and there is no record of whether the manuscripts were given in 1939 or merely catalogued then. Gregg died in 1937.

INTRODUCTION BY FRANK M. GREGG

1. According to the prejudice of the time, white people were considered superior in intelligence to black people.

2. Frank Alexander Stivers (1865–1938) was the son of Andrew Jackson Stivers (1818–94) and Katherine (Maddox) Stivers. Both father and son were in the banking business. Stivers was approximately the same age as Gregg.

3. The age Gregg gives for Parker is not consistent with Chapter 6 of the memoir, in which Parker says that six months after the contract

was made he was eighteen. The widow, Elizabeth Ryder, is listed in the 1838 and 1844 Mobile city directories.

4. The mathematics of the deal are never made entirely clear. In Chapter 6 of the memoir, Parker mentions "payment of $1,800, with interest, to be paid at the rate of $10 per week," but he makes irregular payments and earns his freedom in eighteen months. Possibly the $10 per week was the interest and Parker was to pay off the principal at any rate he could.

5. New Albany, located nearly opposite Louisville, Kentucky, saw its population practically quadruple from 2,079 to 8,181 between 1830 and 1850 as the steamboat and the Portland Canal at Louisville dramatically increased river traffic.

6. Alexander Campbell (1779–1857) was born in Virginia and moved to Kentucky. A doctor, in 1803 he was elected to the state legislature. After moving to Ohio he was elected to the Ohio legislature and served from 1807 to 1809. From 1809 to 1813 he served in the United States Senate, and in 1815 he moved to Ripley to practice medicine. He became vice-president of the first general antislavery society in 1835 and was Ripley's mayor from 1838 to 1840.

7. It was an article of faith among the sons of John Rankin that their father's *Letters to a Slave Holder* was instrumental in lighting a fire under William Lloyd Garrison.

THE AUTOBIOGRAPHY OF JOHN P. PARKER

1. It is interesting that Parker attributes both positive and negative traits to his white father. It is impossible to know if Parker spoke in these terms because of his white audience.

2. The shift of the African-American population from the upper to the lower south was caused not only by the sale of African-American slaves but also by the migration of slave-owning families to the cotton-rich lands of the lower south. By comparison, the loss due to runaways was minor—amounting to perhaps one thousand a year for the nation as a whole and one hundred a year for Kentucky.

3. Slave owners feared that literacy might provoke unrest and even rebellion among slaves.

4. A careful study of Yale catalogs of the period reveals no year when those enrolled included two brothers from Mobile, nor do surnames

of any of the Mobile students, of whom there were a number, match up with surnames of members of the local medical association for 1844. On the other hand, such students would have to pass an examination to get in once they reached New Haven.

5. Natchez had a notorious reputation nationwide.
6. For Mike Fink see Walter Blair and Franklin J. Meine, eds., *Half Horse Half Alligator: The Growth of the Mike Fink Legend* (Chicago, 1956). Mike Fink lived from 1770 to 1823, and his notorious actions became the basis of legends. It would not have been unusual for Parker to hear stories of Mike Fink while he was on the Mississippi.
7. No such steamboat is listed in *Merchant Steam Vessels of the United States—1868: The Lytle-Holdcamper List* as existing at this time, but the list is incomplete.
8. Of all religious groups, Quakers were most likely to aid fugitives.
9. If he learned a trade, a slave might be able to hire himself out for a greater amount than he paid his master for the privilege. In a number of cases such slaves were in time able to purchase their freedom or, if married, first their wife's freedom and later their own. (The offspring of a wife who was free were also free. If the male bought his own freedom first, he would then have to purchase not only his wife's freedom, but also the freedom of all of his children.) The practice is seen as an urban phenomenon but occurred in rural areas as well. Some slaves were rented out to the iron industry at a distance. It was also a method that gave an owner with a surplus of slaves an alternative to selling them. The practice was the norm when children of slave owners became orphans, for the guardian needed cash each year until the children reached their majority.
10. The *Magnolia,* built in 1845, ran the New Orleans–Vicksburg trade and to St. Louis and Louisville off season, as noted in Frederick Way, Jr., *Way's Packet Directory, 1848–1983* (Athens, Ohio, 1983). An 1846 advertisement for the steamer appears in Leonard V. Huber, compiler, *Advertisements of Lower Mississippi River Steamboats 1812–1920* (West Barrington, R.I.: Steamship Historical Society of America, 1959), p. 44.
11. This is an extreme case of contestation of rights. That is, Parker realized that he had no value dead and therefore the white man would not shoot.

12. Parker's experience with and his trust of fellow African-Americans were not unique.

13. Slaves were frequently used in the iron industry in the South. See, for example, Charles B. Dew, *Bond of Iron: Master and Slave at Buffalo Forge* (New York: Norton, 1994); Robert S. Starobin, *Industrial Slavery in the Old South* (New York: Oxford, 1970); and Charles B. Dew, *Ironmaker to the Confederacy: Joseph R. Anderson and the Tredegar Iron Works* (New Haven: Yale, 1966).

14. I could find no listing for Jennings as a foundryman in the 1844 New Orleans city directory.

15. Three gilded balls are the symbol of a pawnshop, used from a time when a large proportion of those who pawned items were illiterate.

16. Parker turned 18 in 1845 and began his work assisting runaway slaves approximately a year later.

17. A steamboat owner was held liable if an escaped slave took passage on his vessel. Consequently passports or free papers were required.

18. Particularly in Kentucky, where masters served in the 1813 campaigns leading to the battles of the Thames and Lake Erie, slaves gained an awareness of Canada.

19. In antebellum times the Ohio River was free-running and its depth and width depended on rainfall and ice gorges. Especially since the 1960s the river has been transformed into a series of lengthy artificial pools. Because the border between Ohio and Kentucky is the historic shoreline of Ohio, we know that at Ripley land extended an additional half block beyond today's boundary. A nineteenth-century atlas shows a similar situation at Maysville, Kentucky.

20. Ripley's Liberty Monument (1912) listed John T. Rankin, James Gilliland, Jesse Lockhart, John B. Mahan, Alfred Beasley, Greenleaf G. Norton, Alexander Campbell, Theodore and Thomas Collins, Samuel Kirkpatrick, Thomas McCague, John Parker, and Col. James Poage as "The Men Who Fought for Liberty."

21. Gregg placed a tablet on the McCague house which, he said, "perhaps delineates the character of Aunt Kitty. This tablet marks the home of Thomas McCague, an ardent antislavery advocate. On one occasion John Parker, an Underground Railroad conductor being pursued, brought a party of slaves to his house at break of day. McCague said, 'It's daylight, don't stop.' His wife, Aunt Kitty, said:

'Daylight or no daylight, Parker, bring them in.' " Eliese Bambach Stivers, *Ripley, Ohio: Its History and Families* (n.p., 1965), p. 25.

22. It is actually a two-story house.

23. Henry Howe, *Historical Collections of Ohio* (Cincinnati: 1902), vol. 2, p. 339, tells a story in which Parker saved the day by aiming his double-barreled shotgun at the intruders, who were about to blow Rankin away.

24. See W. M. Mitchell, *The Underground Railroad by Rev. W. M. Mitchell of Toronto Canada West* (London, 1860), p. 4, as well as Stivers, *Ripley*, p. 25.

25. The Rev. James Gilliland, a 1792 graduate of Dickinson College, preached in South Carolina until dismissed for his antislavery proclivities. He arrived at Red Oak in 1805 and died February 1, 1845. He is buried in the Red Oak Cemetery. Red Oak became a key station on the Underground Railroad.

26. The Rev. Jesse H. Lockhart came from Tennessee. John Rankin set him up at Russellville, Ohio.

27. A number of masters freed slaves, often by means of a will. In some cases such slaves were the offspring of the master's family. Governments feared that such individuals might end up as wards of the state and consequently required bonds. Such a liability could be avoided if the slave was sent to Ohio.

28. Levi Coffin, *Reminiscences* (Cincinnati: 1876), pp. 304, 307–9, mentions a company of 28 and Coffin's ruse of a funeral procession.

29. Samuel Hemphill (1814–79) was born in Pennsylvania. His father died in the War of 1812. His mother brought him to Ohio about 1824, and some eight years later he moved to Ripley, where he became a merchant, married, and had three children.

30. Archibald Leggett was born in Pennsylvania about 1797. A wealthy man, by 1860 he was worth $50,000.

31. Thomas McCague (1793–1864) was an important pork merchant in Ripley.

32. At least thirteen steamboats, all side-wheelers, were built at Ripley. All but the *Caledonia* (1833), whose home port was Pittsburgh, had Cincinnati as a home port.

33. The reference is to an earlier fashion which was now out of style. Andrew Jackson was President 1829–37.

34. Stivers, *Ripley,* 83, quotes from Gregg's unpublished "The Imperial Forest" that "both Thomas McCague and Archibald Leggett were rich enough to send their personal funds to aid New York bankers during the Panic of 1837."

35. At this point, pages 50–53 of the manuscript are missing, but because there is no break in the narrative, this may be mere mispagination.

36. Sixty years is a miscalculation, since the interview's most likely date is before the end of 1889 (see note 10 in the Preface). It is impossible to know if Parker misspoke, or if Gregg copied the date wrong or adjusted it for coherence at some later date.

37. The Fugitive Slave Act permitted slave owners to go into the free states and recover their runaway slaves and made it illegal to assist runaways. (In the manuscript the date is incorrectly given as 1852.) The impact among fugitives living in the north was immediate, as hundreds fled from Ohio, New York, Michigan, and elsewhere to Canada. There was a backflow from Canada to the United States once it became apparent that the law could rarely be successfully enforced.

38. This incident was mentioned earlier in the narrative.

39. Jim Srofe, Sroafe, or Shrofe was the molder, according to Stivers, *Ripley,* p. 26. The 1850 census for Mason County, Kentucky, lists a family named Sroafe.

40. The attorney was probably Archibald Leggett.

41. John Brown led a force against the arsenal at Harpers Ferry, Virginia (later West Virginia), on October 16, 1859. He was captured, tried, and hanged, and considered a martyr by many pro-abolitionist northerners.

42. Harriet Beecher Stowe's *Uncle Tom's Cabin* had an enormous impact on the country. It became a best-seller, and its depiction of slavery seared the national consciousness. She was bitterly assailed in the south while she won the plaudits of abolitionists and other northerners.

43. John Rankin, Jr., the principal source of Gregg's "Eliza of Uncle Tom's Cabin" manuscript, declared that the fall following Eliza's crossing, when he was a student at Lane Seminary, his father told Harriet Beecher Stowe of the incident, and she commented, "Terrible, how terrible." Another son, Richard C. Rankin, in his April 8,

1892, interview with Wilbur H. Siebert, said that the telling occurred at Ripley when the Cincinnati Synod met there soon after the incident.

44. Richard C. Rankin declared that Eliza was from Fleming County; the Rankin manuscript VFM 2137 declared that Eliza's daughter was owned by Thomas Davis "2½ miles back of Dover near Germantown," which would place her in Bracken County or Mason County.

45. Eliza's child is sometimes said to be two years old, though popularly referred to as a baby, not a toddler.

46. Rev. John Rankin in the *Emporia* (Kansas) *News,* January 29, 1875, identifies the man as "an Englishman" while his autobiography (typescript) calls him "an old Scotchman." Richard C. Rankin identifies the locale as at Stony Creek near Asa Anderson's farm opposite Red Oak Creek.

47. The winter of 1838 is the best fit for the incident, as the river was thoroughly iced over.

48. John Rankin, Jr., spoke of a "woolen shawl," and this was corroborated by the first witness he interviewed, Mrs. Chambers Baird; however, Richard C. Rankin speaks of the article as a "little red flannel petticoat" that the ferryman John Crosby found the next day and that indicated to those seeking Eliza that they had made it across. Mrs. Charles Campbell spoke of a "flannel skirt" when asked by Gregg.

49. Chance Shaw, the Ohio patrolman near the mouth of Red Oak Creek, was the man with the outstretched hand, according to John Rankin, Jr. His version is perhaps more poetic than the one in the autobiography: "A rough hand suddenly came out of the black night like a hungry devil and seized her. There was no voice, no presence, just a giant hand laid its weight upon her and held her. It was so sudden and unexpected. The fugitive sank helplessly to the ground with a groan." At that Shaw declared, "Woman, you have won your freedom."

50. The original pages 71–72 of the Parker autobiography manuscript are missing.

51. The quote from Harriet Beecher Stowe is derived directly from Gregg's "Eliza of *Uncle Tom's Cabin,*" and the Parker manuscript is but a vehicle for using this information. Parker had not been in Ohio during the 1830s. All he could know was what he had heard secondhand. One is led to conclude that Gregg was trying to prove the

veracity of the Eliza story even while including his own knowledge in the Parker manuscript.

52. Rankin might well have been worried since Kentucky's legal system was harsher than the federal Fugitive Slave Law (1850) in which six months in prison and a fine of $1,000 were imposed. Kentucky's Register of Prisoners from 1855–1861 lists people who helped slaves escape receiving terms from 5–20 years.

53. Others believe the crossing took place at Cincinnati. See Russel B. Nye, "Eliza Crossing the Ice: A Reappraisal of Sources," *Historical and Philosophical Society of Ohio Bulletin* 7 (1950), 105–12; and Felix J. Koch, "Where Did Eliza Cross the Ohio?" *Ohio Archaeological, Historical and Philosophical Society Quarterly* 25 (1915), 588–90. Nye does not deny Rankin's role, but he looks to the late 1840s, not the 1830s, for the incident.

54. According to Gregg's "Imperial Forest," Parker aided 900 fugitives, including those whom he aided during the war through the recruitment of Union soldiers. The Parker manuscript gives two other figures—315 before he tossed out his memorandum book and 440 when he ended his work.

55. I have been unable to find reference to this reward in the Mason County Circuit Court Order Books. The reward may have been agreed upon by a group of slaveowners.

56. Charleston Bottom Road appears on modern Mason County maps and is about four miles west of Maysville.

57. Parker had little choice in leaving the obese woman behind. Either he endangered the original party and himself, or he attempted the escape including the extra woman, most likely causing all to be captured.

58. One William Robinson, a mulatto born in Tennessee, is listed as a deckhand in the 1860 census of Ripley.

59. Only one Irishman named Tim appears in the naturalization records of Brown County, Ohio. Timothy O'Carrol was naturalized in 1864.